WEBSTER'S
DICTIONARY
OF QUOTATIONS

WEBSTER'S
DICTIONARY
OF QUOTATIONS

Auriel Douglas and Michael Strumpf

GRAMERCY BOOKS

NEW YORK

This 2003 edition is published by Gramercy Books, an imprint of Random House Value Publishing, a division of Random House, Inc., New York, by arrangement with Macmillan Publishing.

Gramercy is a registered trademark and the colophon is a trademark of Random House, Inc.

Random House
New York • Toronto • London • Sydney • Auckland
www.randomhouse.com

Printed and bound in the United States of America

[Previously published as *Webster's New World Dictionary of Quotations*]

Library of Congress Cataloging-in-Publication Data

Douglas, Auriel.
  Webster's dictionary of quotations/Auriel Douglas and Michael Strumpf.
    p. cm.
  Originally published: Webster's New World dictionary of quotations.
    New York: Macmillan, 1998.
  Includes bibliographical references and index.
  ISBN 0-517-22060-1
    1. Quotations, English. 2. Quotations. I Title: Dictionary of
  quotations. II. Strumpf, Michael. III. Douglas, Ariel. Webster's New
  World dictionary of quotations. IV. Title.

PN6081 .W3655 2002

                                             2002070864

10 9 8 7 6 5 4 3 2 1

Table of Contents

Introduction

The purpose of this book is to present quotations that can help the reader reinforce speeches, underline important points, and deliver a brilliant illumination of some obscure point. The words are an eternal legacy; when they were originally spoken or written, the author certainly had little idea that his/her observations would last into the present. Yet here they are, helping to guide us either by solving problems or providing inspiration.

These quotations are bright, pithy, and usable. Delivered by the likes of Goethe, Wilde, Bierce, Butler, Russell, Johnson, Baudelaire, and many others—with a particular emphasis on contemporary sources—they serve to guide us when we can't provide our own wisdom to solve a dilemma, spark a conversation, or fascinate an audience. Their uses are limitless.

The compilers hope that these selections, drawn from all classes of quotations from adages to truisms, will meet the reader's needs and ultimately give pleasure, wisdom, and inspiration. It is also hoped that this book will be a welcome addition to all libraries whether public or private.

The following is a list of the many different classes of quotations and their definitions.

Adage: An old saying that has been popularly accepted as a truth.

Anecdote: A little-known, entertaining fact of history or biography. A short, entertaining account of some happening, usually personal or biographical.

Aphorism: A concise statement of a principle. A short, pointed sentence expressing a wise or clever observation or a general truth; maxim; adage. Synonym: saying.

Apothegm: A short, pithy saying.

Axiom: A statement universally accepted as true; maxim. An established principle or law of a science, art, and so on.

Bromide: A trite saying or statement. Synonym: platitude.

Cliché: An expression or idea that has become trite. Synonym: platitude.

Dictum: A statement or saying; specifically, a formal statement of fact, opinion, principle, or of one's will or judgment; a pronouncement.

Maxim: A concisely expressed principle or rule of conduct, or statement of a general truth. Synonym: saying.

Motto: A word, phrase, or sentence chosen as expressive of the goals or ideals of a nation or group and inscribed on a seal, banner, coin, and so forth.

Platitude: A commonplace or trite remark, especially one uttered as if it were fresh or original.

Proverb: A short saying in common use that expresses some obvious truth or familiar experience; adage; maxim. In the Bible, an enigmatic saying in which a profound truth is cloaked. Synonym: saying.

Quip: A witty or sarcastic remark or reply; jest or gibe.

Saw: An old homely saying that is well-worn by repetition; maxim; proverb. Synonym: saying.

Saying: An adage, proverb, or maxim. The simple, direct term for any pithy expression of wisdom or truth.

Truism: A statement the truth of which is obvious or well-known or commonplace. Synonym: platitude.

Ability

Ability is commonly found to consist mainly in a big degree of solemnity.

Ambrose Bierce

Ability is nothing without opportunity.

Napoleon Bonaparte

To do great work, a man must be very idle as well as very industrious.

Samuel Butler

To measure up to all that is demanded of him, a man must overestimate his capacities.

Johann Wolfgang von Goethe

There is something that is much more scarce, something rarer than ability. It is the ability to recognize ability.

Robert Half

From such crooked wood as that which man is made of, nothing straight can be fashioned.

Edward Hand

Ability

One machine can do the work of fifty ordinary men. No machine can do the work of one extraordinary man.

Elbert Hubbard

We succeed in enterprises which demand the positive qualities we possess, but we excel in those which also make use of our defects.

Alexis de Tocqueville

Talent without genius isn't much, but genius without talent is nothing whatever.

Paul Valéry

They are able because they think they are able.

Virgil

See also ACCOMPLISHMENT, ACHIEVEMENT, JOBS, WORK

Accomplishment

There is always a multitude of reasons both in favor of doing a thing and against doing it. The art of debate lies in presenting them. The art of

life lies in neglecting ninety-nine hundredths of
them.

Anonymous

The test of a vocation is the love of the drudgery
it involves.

Anonymous

No task is a long one but on which one dare not
start. It becomes a nightmare.

Charles Baudelaire

The reward of a thing well done is to have done it.

Ralph Waldo Emerson

For a thing to remain undone nothing more is
needed than to think it done.

Baltasar Gracián

Could we know what men are most apt to
remember, we might know what they are most
apt to do.

Lord Halifax

Accomplishment

Nothing will ever be attempted if all possible objections must be first overcome.

Samuel Johnson

Those that have done nothing in life are not qualified to judge of those that have done little.

Samuel Johnson

Never undertake anything unless you have the heart to ask Heaven's blessing on your undertaking.

Georg Christoph Lichtenberg

We have got but one life here. It pays, no matter what comes after it, to try and do things, to accomplish things in this life and not merely to have a soft and pleasant time.

Theodore Roosevelt

Knowledge may give weight, but accomplishments give luster, and many more people see than weigh.

Philip Stanhope

Men despise great projects when they do not feel themselves capable of great success.

Marquis de Vauvenargues

See also ABILITY, ACHIEVEMENT, FAME, JOBS, WORK

Achievement

There is no such thing as a great talent without great willpower.

Honoré de Balzac

Between vague wavering Capability and fixed indubitable Performance, what a difference!

Thomas Carlyle

If you cannot work with love but only with dis-taste it is better that you should leave your work and sit at the gates of the temple and take alms of those who work with joy.

Khalil Gibran

The man who is born with a talent which he has meant to use finds his greatest happiness in using it.

Johann Wolfgang von Goethe

Every calling is great when greatly pursued.

Oliver Wendell Holmes

The only thing some people do is get older.

Edgar Watson Howe

Achievement

The world is moving so fast these days that the man who says it can't be done is generally interrupted by someone doing it.

Elbert Hubbard

Those who believe that they are exclusively in the right are generally those who achieve something.

Aldous Huxley

Perseverance is a great element of success; if you only knock long enough and loud enough at the gate you are sure to wake up somebody.

Henry Wadsworth Longfellow

We act as though it were our mission to bring about the triumph of truth, but our mission is only to fight for it.

Blaise Pascal

It is, no doubt, an immense advantage to have done nothing, but one should not abuse it.

Antoine de Rivarol

This is the true joy in life, the being used for a purpose recognized by yourself as a mighty one,

the being thoroughly worn out before you are
thrown on the scrap heap, the being a force of
nature instead of a feverish selfish little clod of ail-
ments and grievances complaining that the world
will not devote itself to making you happy.

George Bernard Shaw

The youth gets together his materials to build a
bridge to the moon, or, perchance, a palace or
temple on the earth, and, at length, the middle-
aged man concludes to build a woodshed with
them.

Henry David Thoreau

Discard the old maxim, "Do not get others to do
what you can do yourself." My motto is, do not
do that which others can do as well.

Booker T. Washington

Life is at best only a children's game. Yet the game
must be played conscientiously.

Yukichi

*See also ABILITY, ACCOMPLISHMENT, FAME, JOBS,
WORK*

Acting

An actor is a sculptor who carves in snow.

Barret-Booth

Act singly, and what you have already done singly will justify you now.

Ralph Waldo Emerson

Show me a great actor, and I'll show you a lousy husband. Show me a great actress, and you've seen the devil.

W. C. Fields

You spend all your life trying to do something they put people in asylums for.

Jane Fonda

What acting means is that you've got to get out of your own skin.

Katharine Hepburn

I never said that all actors are cattle; what I said was that all actors should be treated like cattle.

Alfred Hitchcock

Some of the greatest love affairs I've known involved one actor, unassisted.

Wilson Mizner

You say, "Let's get it done real," but acting is just one version of the unreal after another.

Jack Nicholson

Acting is just one big bag of tricks.

Sir Laurence Olivier

We wear the robes that we have designed for ourselves, and then act out other people's fantasies.

Sir Laurence Olivier

Acting is not an important job in the scheme of things. Plumbing is.

Spencer Tracy

You can pick out the actors by the glazed look that comes into their eyes when the conversation wanders away from themselves.

Michael Wilding

See also DRAMA, FILMS, HOLLYWOOD, TALENT, TELEVISION

Action

A person has to be busy to stay alive.

Maxwell Anderson

He who desires, but acts not, breeds pestilence.

William Blake

Action springs not from thought, but from a readiness for responsibility.

Dietrich Bonhoeffer

I believe in living life dangerously; I think a lot of others do too.

Charles, Prince of Wales

To act responsibly, you have to take leaps without being sane.

Daniel Ellsberg

There enters into all human action more luck than judgment.

André Gide

What the hell . . . you might be right; you might be wrong, but don't just avoid.

Katharine Hepburn

Enthusiasm finds the opportunities, and energy makes the most of them.

Henry Hoskins

Act only on that maxim through which you can at the same time will that it should become a universal law.

Immanuel Kant

The absence of alternatives clears the mind marvelously.

Henry Kissinger

Behind many acts that many thought ridiculous, there lie many wise and weighty motives.

François de La Rochefoucauld

What the world needs is some "do give a damn" pills.

William Meninger

All the fun is locking horns with impossibilities.

Claes Oldenburg

Nothing is so exhausting as indecision, and nothing so futile.

Bertrand Russell

Action

Today is your day! Your mountain is waiting. So
... get on your way!

Dr. Seuss

It's easier to fight for one's principles than to live
up to them.

Adlai Stevenson

See also BRAVERY, CONFIDENCE, SUCCESS

Adolescence

Consider well the proportions of things. It is better to be a young June bug than an old bird of
paradise.

Anonymous

I remember my youth and the feeling that will
never come back any more, the feeling that I
could last forever, outlast the sea, the earth, and
all men.

Joseph Conrad

Young fellows are tempted by girls; men who are
thirty years old are tempted by gold; when they
are forty years old, they are tempted by honor and

glory, and those who are sixty years old, say to themselves, "What a pious man I have become."

Martin Luther

The childhood shews the man as morning shews the day.

John Milton

Maybe more youngsters would stay home nights if they weren't afraid to stay alone in the house.

Herbert Prochnow

Old places and old persons in their turn, when spirit dwells in them, have an intrinsic vitality of which youth is incapable, precisely, the balance and wisdom that come from long perspectives and broad foundations.

George Santayana

My salad days,
When I was green in judgment, cold in blood, to say as I
said then.

William Shakespeare: Antony and Cleopatra

Adolescence

Crabbed age and youth cannot live together;
Youth is full of pleasance, age is full of care. Youth
like summer morn; age like winter weather; youth
like summer brave; age like winter bear; youth is
full of sport; age's breath is short; youth is nimble;
age is lame; youth is hot, and old age is weak and
cold; youth is wild, and age is tame; age, I do
abhor thee; youth, I do adore thee.

William Shakespeare: The Passionate Pilgrim

Then come kiss me, sweet and twenty, youth's a
stuff will not endure.

William Shakespeare: Sonnets

I have no contempt for that time of life when our
friendships are most passionate and our passions are
incorrigible and none of our sentiments yet com-
promised by greed or cowardice or disappointment.

Edmund White

In America, the young are always ready to give to
those that are older than themselves the full benefits of their inexperience.

Oscar Wilde

See also AGE, CHILDREN, YOUTH

Advertising

You can tell the ideals of a nation by its advertisements.

Norman Douglas

It is not necessary to advertise food to hungry people, fuel to cold people, or houses to the homeless.

John Kenneth Galbraith

Advertisements contain the only truth to be relied on in the newspaper.

Thomas Jefferson

Advertising may be described as the science of arresting the human intelligence long enough to get money from it.

Stephen Leacock

Advertising is the rattling of a stick inside a swill bucket.

George Orwell

Advertising

Let advertisers spend the same amount of money improving their product as they do on advertising, and they wouldn't have to advertise it.

Will Rogers

Advertising is the art of making whole lies out of half-truths.

Edgar Shoaff

Invention is the mother of necessity.

Thorstein Veblen

Advertising is legalized lying.

H. G. Wells

Advice

Never trust the advice of a man in difficulties.

Aesop

To ask for advice is, in nine cases out of ten, to tout for flattery.

Anonymous

We hate those who will not take our advice and despise those who do.

Josh Billings

In giving advice, I advise you, be short.

Horace

A good scare is worth more to a man than good advice.

Edgar Watson Howe

Advice is what we ask for when we already know the answer but wish we didn't.

Erica Jong

Old people like to give good advice, as solace for no longer being able to provide bad examples.

François de La Rochefoucauld

"Be yourself" is about the worst advice you can give to people.

Tom Masson

Only when a man is safely ensconced under six feet of earth, with several tons of . . . granite upon his chest, is he in a position to give advice with any certainty, and then he is silent.

A. Edward Newton

How is it possible to expect that mankind will take advice when they will not so much as take warning.

Jonathan Swift

I have lived some thirty-odd years on this planet and I have yet to hear the first syllable of valuable or even earnest advice from my seniors.

Henry David Thoreau

I have found the best way to give advice to your children is to find out what they want and then advise them to do it.

Harry Truman

Don't give a woman advice; one should never give a woman anything she can't wear in the evening.

Oscar Wilde

I always pass on good advice. It is the only thing to do with it. It is never of any use to oneself.

Oscar Wilde

It is always a silly thing to give advice, but to give good advice is fatal.

Oscar Wilde

See also CRITICISM, TRUTH

African-Americans

A racially integrated community is a chronological term timed from the entrance of the first black family to the exit of the last white family.

Saul Alinsky

The man ain't prejudiced. He doesn't care what color his slaves are.

C. Anderson

Say it loud! I'm black and I'm proud!

James Brown

To like an individual because he's black is just as insulting as to dislike him because he isn't white.

e. e. cummings

African-Americans

Some people have a wonderful way of looking at things. Like the ones who hire us to baby-sit so they can go to a Ku Klux Klan meeting.

Dick Gregory

The American nation ought to be ashamed of themselves for letting their medals be won by Negroes.

Adolf Hitler

The burden of being black is that you have to be superior to be equal. But the glory of it is that once you have achieved you have achieved indeed!

Jesse Jackson

I want to be the white man's brother, not his brother-in-law.

Martin Luther King, Jr.

To be young, gifted and black
Is where it's at!

Nina Simone

There are those who believe black people possess the secret of joy and that this will sustain them through any spiritual or moral or physical devastation.

Alice Walker

If they really believe there is danger from the Negro, it must be because they do not intend to give him justice.

Booker T. Washington

You can't hold a man down without staying down with him.

Booker T. Washington

I believe in white supremacy until the blacks are educated to a point of responsibility.

John Wayne

See also PREJUDICE, RACE and RACISM

Afterlife

Good Americans, when they die, go to Paris.

Thomas Gold Appleton

Ah, but a man's reach should exceed his grasp,
Or what's a heaven for?

Robert Browning

21

Afterlife

Parting is all we know of heaven,
And all we need of hell.

Emily Dickinson

Many might go to heaven with half the labor they
go to hell.

Ralph Waldo Emerson

To reach the port of heaven, we must sail sometimes, with the wind and sometimes against it—
but we must sail, and not drift, nor lie at anchor.

Oliver Wendell Holmes

Is there another life? Shall I awake and find this
all a dream? There must be; we cannot be created
for this type of suffering.

John Keats

The great world of light that lies
Behind all human destinies.

Henry Wadsworth Longfellow

The heavens declare the glory of God; and the
firmament showeth his handiwork.

Psalms 19:1

God will often say to us, "You are not in Heaven for fun!"

Jules Renard

I can believe anything, but the justice of this world does not give me a very reassuring idea of the justice in the next. I am very much afraid that God will go on blundering; he will receive the wicked in paradise and hurl the good into hell.

Jules Renard

God is growing bitter. He envies man his mortality.

Jacques Rigaut

After your death, you will be what you were before your birth.

Arthur Schopenhauer

We feel and know that we are eternal.

Baruch Spinoza

What they do in heaven, we are ignorant of. What they do not do we are told expressly.

Jonathan Swift

Afterlife

Heaven goes by favor, if it went by merit, you would stay out, and your dog would go in.

Mark Twain

What a man misses most in heaven is company.

Mark Twain

When bad Americans die, they go to America.

Oscar Wilde

See also BIBLE, CHRISTIANITY, DEATH, ETERNITY, GOD, HELL, RELIGION

Age

Age is deformed, youth unkind. We scorn their bodies, they, our mind.

Anonymous

Do not regret growing older, it's a privilege denied to many.

Anonymous

Old men are children for a second time.

Aristophanes

Age

A man of sixty has spent twenty years in bed and over three years in eating.

Arnold Bennett

At fifty, a man's real life begins. He has acquired upon which to achieve, received from which to give, learned from which to teach, learned upon which to build.

Derek Bok

Old age takes away from us what we have inherited and gives us what we have earned.

Gerald Brenan

Grow old along with me!
The best is yet to be . . .

Robert Browning

There is nothing sadder than an old hipster.

Lenny Bruce

For time it is, age has great advantages; experience and wisdom come with age. Men may be old outrun, but not outwit.

Geoffrey Chaucer

Age

Getting married and getting old are the two things that save everybody's ass.

Cher

Old age is not so bad when you consider the alternative.

Maurice Chevalier

No man is so old as to think he cannot live one more year.

Cicero

When you become senile, you won't know it.

Bill Cosby

We do not count a man's years until he has nothing else to count.

Ralph Waldo Emerson

If youth but knew, if old age but could.

Henri Estienne

Setting a good example for your children takes all the fun out of middle age.

William Feather

Maturity is only a short break in adolescence.

Jules Feiffer

It is magnificent to grow old if one keeps young.

Harry Emerson Fosdick

Old age is a shipwreck.

Charles de Gaulle

There are only three ages for women in
Hollywood: babe, district attorney, and Driving
Miss Daisy.

Goldie Hawn

Gather ye rosebuds while ye may,
Old time is still aflying.

Robert Herrick

The longer thread of life we spin, the more occasion still to sin.

Robert Herrick

Forty is the old age of youth; fifty is the youth of
old age.

Victor Hugo

Age

There are few things that are so unwilling given up, even in advanced age, as the supposition that we have still the power of ingratiating ourselves with the fair sex.

Samuel Johnson

Youth has been a habit of hers for so long that she could not part with it.

Rudyard Kipling

I go back so far I'm in front of me.

Paul McCartney

Age is not all decay; it is the ripening, the swelling, of the fresh life within, that withers and bursts the husks.

George MacDonald

Middle age is the time when a man is always thinking that in a week or two he will feel as good as ever.

Don Marquis

We look forward to a disorderly, vigorous, unhonored, and disreputable old age.

Don Marquis

Anyone can get old; all you have to do is to live long enough.

Groucho Marx

The best years are the forties. After fifty, a man begins to deteriorate, but in the forties he is at the maximum of his villainy.

H. L. Mencken

Old age puts more wrinkles in our minds than on our faces, and we never, or rarely, see a soul that in growing old does not come to smell sour and musty. Man grows and dwindles in his entirety.

Ashley Montague

Men are like wine; some turn to vinegar, but the best improve with age.

Pope John XXIII

Unfortunately, man never gets too old or too experienced to be stupid in some new way.

Herbert Prochnow

When I was young, I used to say good-natured things, and nobody listened to me. Now that I am old, I say ill-natured things, and everybody listens to me.

Samuel Rogers

As you grow older, you'll find the only things you regret are the things you didn't do.

Zachary Scott

Nothing so dates a man as to decry the younger generation.

Adlai Stevenson

I think age is a very high price to pay for maturity.

Tom Stoppard

Old age is the night of life, as night is the old age of the day. Still night is full of magnificence and, for many, it is more brilliant than the day.

Anne Sophie Swetchine

No wise man ever wished to be younger.

Jonathan Swift

For the unlearned, old age is winter; for the learned it is the season of the harvest.

The Talmud

The Peace Corps is sort of a Howard Johnson's
on the main drag to maturity.

Paul Theroux

Dawn comes slowly, but dusk is rapid.

Alice B. Toklas

I am not young enough to know everything.

Oscar Wilde

See also ADOLESCENCE, CHILDREN, LIFE, TIME

Alcohol

When you stop drinking, you have to deal with
this marvelous personality that started you drinking in the first place.

Jimmy Breslin

I have always taken more out of alcohol than
alcohol has taken out of me.

Winston Churchill

A man is never drunk if he can lay on the floor
without holding on.

Joe E. Lewis

Alcohol

I always wake up at the crack of ice.

Joe E. Lewis

If you drink like a fish, don't drive. Swim.

Joe E. Lewis

In wine, there is truth.

Pliny the Elder

Of all vices, drinking is the most incompatible with greatness.

Sir Walter Scott

The worst thing about some men is that when they are drunk they are sober.

William Butler Yeats

See also DESPERATION, EMPTINESS

Alimony

Alimony is like buying oats for a dead horse.

Arthur Baer

You never realize how short a month is until you pay alimony.

John Barrymore

I don't think I'll get married again. I'll just find a woman I don't like and give her a house.

Lewis Grizzard

She cried and the judge wiped her tears with my checkbook.

Tommy Manville

See also DIVORCE, MARRIAGE

Ambition

I had ambition not only to go farther than any man had been before, but as far as it was possible for a man to go.

Joseph Cook

One can never consent to creep when one feels an impulse to soar.

Helen Keller

Women who seek to be equal to men lack ambition.

Timothy Leary

Ambition

Aim at heaven and you will get earth thrown in.
Aim at earth and you will get neither.

C. S. Lewis

Ours is a world where people don't know what
they want and are willing to go through hell to
get it.

Don Marquis

Everybody sets out to do something, and everybody does something, but no one does what he
sets out to do.

George Moore

There's always something to suggest that you'll
never be who you wanted to be. Your choice is to
take it or keep on moving.

Phylicia Rashad

Ambition is like hunger; it obeys no law but its
appetite.

Herbert Shaw

Ambition often puts men upon doing the meanest offices: so climbing is performed in the same
posture with creeping.

Jonathan Swift

Keep away from people who try to belittle your ambitions. Small people always do that, but the really great make you feel that you, too, can become great.

Mark Twain

See also WORK

Americans

America is the only country where you buy a lifetime supply of aspirin and use it up in two weeks.

John Barrymore

Only Americans can hurt America.

Dwight D. Eisenhower

Americans are like a rich father, who wishes he knew how to give his sons the hardships that made him rich.

Robert Frost

I don't know why vigor went out of America and why a con man blandness replaced it.

Ben Hecht

Americans

Intellectually, I know that America is no better than any other country. Emotionally, I know she is better than every other country.

Sinclair Lewis

Americans are much as the Greeks found the Romans—great big, vulgar, bustling people more vigorous . . . more ideal . . . with more unspoiled virtues, but also more corrupt.

Harold Macmillan

The American people never carry an umbrella. They prepare to walk in eternal sunshine.

Al Smith

America is a large friendly dog in a small room. Every time it wags its tail, it knocks over a chair.

Arnold Toynbee

America had often been discovered before Columbus, but it had always been hushed up.

Oscar Wilde

A man who thinks of himself as belonging to a particular national group in America has not yet become an American.

Woodrow Wilson

See also ENGLISH

Ancestry

Snobs talk as if they had forgotten their ancestors.

Horatio Alger

Once in every half century, at longest, a family should be merged into the great obscure mass of humanity and forget all about its ancestors.

Nathaniel Hawthorne

None of us can boast about the morality of our ancestors. The records do not show that Adam and Eve were married.

Edgar Watson Howe

There is no king who has not had a slave amongst his ancestors, and no slave who has not had a king among his.

Helen Keller

Ancestry

She is descended from a long line her mother
listened to.

Gypsy Rose Lee

I don't know who my grandfather was; I am
much more concerned to know what his grand-
son will be.

Abraham Lincoln

It is indeed desirable to be well descended, but
the glory belongs to our ancestors.

Plutarch

My folks didn't come over on the *Mayflower*, but
they were there to meet the boat.

Will Rogers

If you cannot get rid of the family skeleton, you
may as well make it dance.

George Bernard Shaw

Genealogist: one who traces back your family as
far as your money will go.

Oscar Wilde

See also FAMILY, PARENTS

Anger

How much more grievous are the consequences of anger than the causes of it.

Marcus Aurelius

Never forget what a man has said to you when he was angry.

Henry Ward Beecher

Personal relations are the important thing for ever and ever, and not this outer life of telegrams and anger.

E. M. Forster

Anger is never without an argument, but seldom with a good one.

Lord Halifax

Anger blows out the lamp of the mind.

Robert Ingersoll

To be angry is to revenge the faults of others upon ourselves.

Alexander Pope

Anger

Think when you are enraged at anyone, what would probably become your sentiments should he die during the dispute.

William Shenstone

Anger always thinks it has power beyond its power.

Publilius Syrus

When angry, count four; when very angry, swear.

Mark Twain

A hurtful act is the transference to others of the degradation which we bear in ourselves.

Simone Weil

See also ARGUMENT, FEELINGS, WAR

Animals

All animals except man know that the ultimate in life is to enjoy it.

Samuel Butler

Mankind differs from the animals only by a little, and most people throw that away.

Confucius

I distrust camels, and anyone else who can go a
week without a drink.

Joe E. Lewis

Men are the only animals that devote themselves,
day in and day out to making one another happy.

H. L. Mencken

Behind each beautiful wild fur, there is an ugly
story. It is a brutal, bloody and barbaric story. The
animal is not killed, it is tortured. I don't think a
fur coat is worth it.

Mary Tyler Moore

If modern civilized man had to keep the animals
he eats, the number of vegetarians would rise
astronomically.

Christian Morgenstern

All animals are equal, but some animals are more
equal than others.

George Orwell

I have always thought of a dog lover as a dog that
was in love with another dog.

James Thurber

Animals

We hope that when the insects take over the world, they will remember with gratitude how we took them along on our picnics.

Billy Vaughn

Animals have these advantages over man; they have no theologians to instruct them; their funerals cost them nothing, and no one starts lawsuits over their wills.

Voltaire

See also CATS, DOGS

Argument

It is labor in vain to dispute with a man unless somebody be in company to whose judgment you would both submit.

Anonymous

If you go in for argument, take care of your temper. Your logic, if you have any, will take care of itself.

Joseph Farrell

I never make the mistake of arguing with people
for whose opinions I have no respect.

Edward Gibbon

There is no arguing with Johnson: for if his pistol
misses fire, he knocks you down with the butt
end of it.

Oliver Goldsmith

If you can't answer a man's arguments, all is not
lost; you can still call him vile names.

Elbert Hubbard

You raise your voice when you should reinforce
your argument.

Samuel Johnson

When you argue with your inferiors, you convince
them of only one thing: they are as clever as you.

Irving Layton

Discussion is an exchange of knowledge, argument an exchange of ignorance.

Robert Quillen

Argument

There is no more sense in having an argument with a man so stupid he doesn't know you have the better of him.

John Roper

Before you contradict an old man, my fair friend, you should endeavor to understand him.

George Santayana

I dislike arguments of any kind. They are always vulgar and often convincing.

Oscar Wilde

See also ANGER

The Arts

To do easily what is difficult for others is the mark of talent. To do what is impossible for talent is the mark of genius.

Henri-Frédéric Amiel

Life is more important than art; that's what makes art important.

James Baldwin

It is as easy to dream a book as it is hard to write one.

Honoré de Balzac

Art is I; science is we.

Claude Bernard

If Shakespeare had to go on an author tour to promote Romeo and Juliet, he never would have written Macbeth.

Dr. Joyce Brothers

Abstract art is a product of the untalented, sold by the unprincipled, to the utterly bewildered.

Al Capp

Art is nature speeded up, and God slowed down.

M. Chazal

Immature poets imitate; mature poets steal.

T. S. Eliot

Of all lies, art is the least untrue.

Gustave Flaubert

The Arts

Art is uncompromising, and life is full of compromises.

Günter Grass

The important thing is not what the author, or any artist, had in mind to begin with but at what point he decided to stop.

D. W. Harding

The rule in the art world is you cater to the masses, or you kowtow to the elite; you can't have both.

Ben Hecht

Only a person with a Best Seller mind can write Best Sellers.

Aldous Huxley

The structure of a play is always the story of how the birds came home to roost.

Arthur Miller

A primitive artist is an amateur whose work sells.

Grandma Moses

For art to exist, for any sort of aesthetic activity or perception to exist, a certain physiological precondition is indispensable; intoxication.

Friedrich Wilhelm Nietzsche

I paint objects as I think them, not as I see them.

Pablo Picasso

The perfection of art is to conceal art.

Quintilian

What garlic is to salad, insanity is to art.

Augustus Saint-Gaudens

If it is art, it is not for all, and if it is for all, it is not for art.

Arnold Schoenberg

A poet looks at the world as a man looks at a woman.

Wallace Stevens

Publicity often seems to be about all that is left of the arts.

Igor Stravinsky

The Arts

The painter should not paint what he sees, but what will be seen.

Paul Valéry

I think having land and not ruining it is the most beautiful art that anybody could ever want to own.

Andy Warhol

Any authentic work of art must start an argument between an artist and his audience.

Rebecca West

Art happens—no hovel is safe from it, no prince may depend upon it, the vastest intelligence cannot bring it about.

James McNeill Whistler

Bad artists always admire each other's work.

Oscar Wilde

See also BOOKS, CREATIVITY, MUSIC

Authors

I love being a writer. What I can't stand is the paperwork.

Anonymous

Literary success of any enduring kind is made by refusing to do what publishers want, by refusing to write what the public wants, by refusing to accept any popular standard, by refusing to write anything to order.

Anonymous

It took me fifteen years to discover I had no talent for writing, but I couldn't give it up because by that time I was too famous.

Nathaniel Benchley

Only a small minority of authors overwrite themselves. Most of the good and the tolerable ones do not write enough.

Arnold Bennett

Remember, writers are always selling somebody out.

Joan Didion

Authors

The author who speaks about his own books is almost as bad as the mother who talks about her own children.

Benjamin Disraeli

Everything goes by the board: honor, pride, decency, security, happiness, all, to get the book written. If a writer has to rob his mother, he will not hesitate.

William Faulkner

Your manuscript is both good and original, but the part that is good is not original, and the part that is original is not good.

Samuel Johnson

The earliest poets and authors made fools wise. Modern authors try to make wise men fools.

Joseph Joubert

When audiences come to see us authors lecture, it is largely in the hope that we'll be funnier to look at than to read.

Sinclair Lewis

From the moment I picked your book up, to the moment I laid it down, I was convulsed with laughter; some day I intend to read it.

Groucho Marx

Writing a book is not as tough as it is to haul thirty-five people around the country and sweat like a horse five nights a week.

Bette Midler

Almost anyone can be an author; the business is to collect money and fame from this state of being.

A. A. Milne

The secret of popular writing is never to put more on a given page than the common reader can lap off it with no strain whatsoever on his habitually slack attention.

Ezra Pound

A pin has as much head on it as some authors and a good deal more point.

George Prentice

Authors

Writing is the only profession where no one considers you ridiculous if you earn no money.

Jules Renard

You must not suppose, because I am a man of letters, that I never tried to earn an honest living.

George Bernard Shaw

Writing is not a profession but a vocation of unhappiness.

Georges Simenon

With sixty staring me in the face, I have developed inflammation of the sentence structure and a definite hardening of the paragraphs.

James Thurber

No one can write decently who is distrustful of the reader's intelligence or whose attitude is patronizing.

E. B. White

See also BOOKS, EDUCATION, LEARNING, LETTERS, LITERATURE, READING, WORDS

Bachelors

It is a truth universally acknowledged, that a single man in possession of a good fortune, must be in want of a wife.

Jane Austen

The only good husbands stay bachelors; they are too considerate to get married.

Finley Peter Dunne

Jesus was a bachelor.

Don Herold

Bachelors know more about women than married men. If they didn't they'd be married too.

H. L. Mencken

A bachelor is one who thinks one can live as cheap as two.

Elizabeth Ridley

A bachelor never quite gets over the idea that he is a thing of beauty and a boy forever.

Helen Rowland

Bachelors

The world must be peopled. When I said I would die a bachelor, I did not think I should live till I were married.

William Shakespeare: Much Ado About Nothing

Call no man unhappy until he's married.

Socrates

By persistently remaining single, a man converts himself into a permanent public temptation.

Oscar Wilde

See also HUSBANDS, MAN, MARRIAGE

Bargains

Necessity never made a good bargain.

Benjamin Franklin

What costs little is little worth.

Baltasar Gracián

One of the difficult tasks in this world is to convince a woman that even a bargain costs money.

Edgar Watson Howe

A woman will buy anything she thinks the store is losing money on.

Kin (Frank McKinney) Hubbard

A bargain is something you can't use but which is so cheap you can't afford not to buy it.

Herbert Prochnow

Marriage is a bargain. And somebody has to get the worst of a bargain.

Helen Rowland

Beauty

In the eyes of a lover, pockmarks are dimples.

Anonymous

Rome was a poem pressed into service as a city.

Anatole Broyard

Everything beautiful has its moments and then passes away.

Luis Cernuda

Beauty

A beautiful woman is paradise for the eyes, hell for soul, and purgatory for the purse.

Nicolas Chamfort

A beautiful woman with a brain is like a beautiful woman with a club foot.

Bernard Cornfeld

We live only to discover beauty. All else is a form of waiting.

Khalil Gibran

The copy of a beautiful thing is always an ugly thing. It is an act of cowardice in admiration of an act of energy.

Rémy de Gourmont

Beauty is not an easy thing to measure. It does not show up in the gross national product, in a weekly paycheck, or in profit-and-loss statements. But these things are not ends in themselves. They are a road to satisfaction and pleasure and the good life. Beauty makes its own direct contribution to these final ends. Therefore it is one of the most important components of our true national income, not to be left out simply because statisticians cannot calculate its worth.

Lyndon Johnson

People who are very beautiful make their own laws.

Vivien Leigh

Beauty without grace is a hook without bait.

Ninon de L'Enclos

Beauty is how you feel inside, and it reflects in your eyes. It is not something physical.

Sophia Loren

Remember that the most beautiful things in the world are the most useless: peacocks and lilies for instance.

John Ruskin

The saying that beauty is but skin deep is but a skin-deep saying.

Herbert Spencer

There are many beautiful things, but the silent beauty of a flower surpasses them all.

S. Teshigahara

Beauty

The only way to behave to a woman is to make love to her if she is pretty and to someone else if she is plain.

Oscar Wilde

The inappropriate cannot be beautiful.

Frank Lloyd Wright

See also CONCEIT

Behavior

He who takes a stand is often wrong, but he who fails to take a stand is always wrong.

Anonymous

Execute every act of thy life as though it were thy last.

Marcus Aurelius

We are all capable of evil thoughts, but only rarely of evil deeds. We can all do good deeds but very few of us can think good thoughts.

Brese

Treat people as if they were what they ought to be and you help them to become what they are capable of being.

Johann Wolfgang von Goethe

Almost all absurdity of conduct arises from the imitation of those whom we cannot resemble.

Samuel Johnson

Therefore all things whatsoever ye would that men should do to you, do ye even so to them . . .

Matthew 7:12

There are some people who are very resourceful at being resourceful and who apparently feel that the best way to make friends is to do something terrible and then to make amends.

Ogden Nash

Nothing prevents our being natural as the desire to seem so.

Arthur Schopenhauer

Few things are harder to put up with than the annoyance of a good example.

Mark Twain

Behavior

We think in generalities, but we live in detail.

Alfred North Whitehead

See also CHARACTER, MAN, MANNERS, SELF

Beliefs

He does not believe that does not live according to his belief.

Thomas Fuller

The more faithfully you listen to the voice within you, the better you will hear what is sounding outside. And only he who listens can speak.

Dag Hammarskjöld

Irrationally held truths may be more harmful than reasoned errors.

Thomas Henry Huxley

Those who never retract their opinions love themselves more than they love the truth.

Joseph Joubert

With most men, unbelief in one thing springs from blind belief in another.

Georg Christoph Lichtenberg

Many a time I have wanted to stop talking and find out what I really believed.

Walter Lippmann

Convictions are more dangerous enemies of truth than lies.

Friedrich Wilhelm Nietzsche

Man is a credulous animal, and must believe something; in the absence of good grounds for belief, he will be satisfied with bad ones.

Bertrand Russell

What a man thinks of himself, that it is which determines, or rather indicates, his fate.

Henry David Thoreau

There is nothing that fear nor hope does not make men believe.

Marquis de Vauvenargues

I can believe anything provided it is incredible.

Oscar Wilde

Fact of the matter is, there is no hip world, there is no straight world. There's a world, you see, which has people in it who believe in a variety of

Beliefs

different things. Everybody believes in something and everybody, by virtue of the fact that they believe in something, uses that something to support their own existence.

Frank Zappa

See also BIBLE, CHRISTIANITY, CONVICTIONS, GOD, IDEALS, TRUST

Bible

In all my perplexities and distresses, the Bible has never failed to give me light and strength.

Anonymous

Scriptures are the sacred books of our holy religion, as distinguished from the false and profane writings on which all other faiths are based.

Ambrose Bierce

The Bible tells us to love our neighbors and also to love our enemies, probably because they are generally the same people.

G. K. Chesterton

The scriptures teach us the best way of living, the noblest way of suffering, and the most comfortable way of dying.

John Flavel

It is impossible to enslave mentally or socially a Bible-reading people. The principles of the Bible are the groundwork of human freedom.

Horace Greeley

The dogma of the infallibility of the Bible is no more self-evident than in the infallibility of the Pope.

Thomas Henry Huxley

The inspiration of the Bible depends on the ignorance of the gentleman who reads it.

Robert Ingersoll

That book, sir, is the rock on which our republic rests.

Andrew Jackson

A knowledge of the Bible without a college course is more valuable than a college course without the Bible.

William Lyon Phelps

Bible

The words of the prophets are written on the subway walls and tenement halls.

Paul Simon

Nobody ever outgrows scripture; the book widens and deepens with our years.

Charles Spurge

I have read the Bible carefully and if Bob Ingersoll isn't in hell, God is a liar and the Bible isn't worth the paper it is printed on.

Billy Sunday

See also AFTERLIFE, BELIEFS, CHRISTIANITY, ETERNITY, FAITH, GOD, HELL, MORALITY

Blame

If you hear that someone is speaking ill of you, instead of trying to defend yourself, you should say: "He obviously does not know me very well, since there are so many other faults he could have mentioned."

Epictetus

Those see nothing but faults that seek for nothing else.

Thomas Fuller

People say ill-natured things without design, but not without having a pleasure in it.

William Hazlitt

If we had no faults of our own we would not take so much pleasure in noticing those of others.

François de La Rochefoucauld

The emphasis in sound discipline must be on *what's wrong*, rather than *who's to blame*.

George Odiorne

To show resentment at a reproach is to acknowledge that one may have deserved it.

Tacitus

The dead are indifferent to slander, but the living can die of it.

Voltaire

Blame

There is luxury in self-reproach. When we blame ourselves, we feel no one else has a right to blame us.

Oscar Wilde

See also DEPRECATION, FORGIVING

Blindness

If thou art a master, be sometimes blind, if a servant, sometimes deaf.

Thomas Fuller

You are blind, and I am deaf and dumb, so let us touch hands and understand.

Khalil Gibran

Be willing to have it so. Acceptance of what has happened is the first step to overcoming the consequences of any misfortune.

William James

I can see, and that is why I can be so happy in what you call the dark, but which to me is golden. I can see a God-made world, not a man-made world.

Helen Keller

Never bend your head. Always hold it high. Look the world straight in the face.

Helen Keller

There's none so blind as they that won't see.

Jonathan Swift

Blushing

The blush is beautiful, but it is sometimes inconvenient.

Carlo Goldoni

There's a blush for won't, and a blush for shan't,
And a blush for having done it;
There's a blush for thought and a blush for nought,
And a blush for just begun it.

John Keats

Men blush less for their crimes than for their weaknesses and vanity.

Jean de La Bruyère

Innocence is not accustomed to blush.

Molière

Blushing

Man is the only animal that blushes. Or needs to.

Mark Twain

The man that blushes is not quite a brute.

Edward Young

Body

When one shuts one eye, one does not hear everything.

Anonymous

The head sublime, the heart pathos, the genitals beauty, hands and feet proportion.

William Blake

We speak with our lips to explain, with our throats to convince.

M. Chazal

One's eyes are what one is, one's mouth what one becomes.

John Galsworthy

The body says what words cannot.

Martha Graham

The eyes and ears are bad mistresses for men, if they have barbarous souls.

Heraclitus

Grace is to the body what clear thinking is to the mind.

François de La Rochefoucauld

The body is a thing. The soul is also a thing. Man is not a thing, but a drama.

José Ortega y Gasset

See also HEALTH

Books

A book is like a garden carried in the pocket.

Anonymous

Solomon made a book of proverbs, but a book of proverbs never made a Solomon.

Anonymous

Some books are undeservedly forgotten; none are undeservedly remembered.

W. H. Auden

Books

When I am dead, I hope it may be said: "His sins were scarlet, but his books were read."

Hilaire Belloc

Books are not men, and yet they are alive.

Stephen Vincent Benét

A best-seller was a book which somehow sold well simply because it was selling well.

Seymour Boorstein

One of the marks of a great poet is that he creates his own family of words and teaches them to live together in harmony and to help one another.

Gerald Brenan

Manuscript: something submitted in haste and returned at leisure.

Lewis Carroll

A room without books is a body without soul.

Cicero

A true poet does not bother to be poetical. Nor does a nursery gardener scent his roses.

Jean Cocteau

A man may as well expect to grow stronger by always eating as wiser by always reading.

David Collier

There is more treasure in books than in all the pirate's loot on Treasure Island, and best of all, you can enjoy these riches every day of your life.

Walt Disney

If we encounter a man of rare intellect we should ask him what books he reads.

Ralph Waldo Emerson

I suggest that the only books that influence us are those for which we are ready and which have gone a little farther down our particular path than we have gone ourselves.

C. S. Forester

Never lend books, for no one ever returns them. The only books I have in my library are those that other folk have lent me.

Anatole France

The most beautiful things are those that madness prompts and reason writes.

André Gide

Books

Some books seem to have been written not to teach us anything but to let us know that the author has known something.

Johann Wolfgang von Goethe

Every work of art adheres to some system of morality. But if it be really a work of art, it must contain the essential criticism of the morality to which it adheres.

D. H. Lawrence

No book is really worth reading at the age of ten which is not equally, and often far more, worth reading at the age of fifty and beyond.

C. S. Lewis

A book is a mirror; if an ass peers into it you can't expect an apostle to peer out.

Georg Christoph Lichtenberg

There are two kinds of books, those that no one reads and those that no one ought to read.

H. L. Mencken

There is hardly any grief that an hour's reading will not dissipate.

Baron de Montesquieu

Read books should be the offspring not of daylight and casual talk but of darkness and silence.

Marcel Proust

To expect a man to retain everything that he has ever read is like expecting him to carry about in his body everything he has ever eaten.

Arthur Schopenhauer

The road to ignorance is paved with good editors.

George Bernard Shaw

How vain it is to sit down to write when you have not stood up to live.

Henry David Thoreau

Youth is a time when we find the books we give up but do not get over.

Lionel Trilling

Books

A classic is something that everyone wants to have read and nobody wants to read.

Mark Twain

We live in an age that reads too much to be wise.

Oscar Wilde

I would never read a book if it were possible for me to talk half an hour with the man who wrote it.

Woodrow Wilson

Neither Christ nor Buddha nor Socrates wrote a book, for to do that is to exchange life for a logical process.

William Butler Yeats

See also AUTHORS, EDUCATION, KNOWLEDGE, LANGUAGE, LEARNING, LETTERS, LITERATURE, READING, WORDS

Boredom

The great advantage of being in a rut is that when one is in a rut, one knows exactly where one is.

Arnold Bennett

Society is now one polish'd horde,
Formed of two mighty tribes, the Bores and Bored.

Lord Byron

Boredom is the most horrible of wolves.

Jean Giono

Boredom is one face of death.

Julian Green

It is a sad truth that everyone is a bore to someone.

L. Miller

Boredom is a vital problem for the moralist since
half the sins of mankind are caused by fear of it.

Bertrand Russell

One can be bored until boredom becomes a mystical experience.

Logan Pearsall Smith

I sometimes say to myself: "Life is too short to be
worth troubling about." Yet if a bore calls on me,
prevents me from going out or attending to my
affairs, I lose patience and cannot endure it for
half an hour.

Marquis de Vauvenargues

Boredom

Punctuality is the virtue of the bored.

Evelyn Waugh

In heaven, they will bore you; in hell, you will bore them.

Katherine Whitehorn

Risk is what separates the good part of life from the tedium.

J. Zero

Bravery

For those who will fight bravely and not yield, there is triumphant victory over all the dark things of life.

J. Allen

One isn't necessarily born with courage, but one is born with potential. Without courage, we cannot practice any other virtue with consistency. We can't be kind, true, merciful, generous or honest.

Maya Angelou

Expect victory and you make victory. Nowhere is this truer than in business life where bravery and faith bring both material and spiritual rewards.

Preston Bradley

Patience and fortitude conquer all things.

Ralph Waldo Emerson

Many would be coward if they had courage enough.

Thomas Fuller

It's not life that counts but the fortitude you bring into it.

John Galsworthy

I am the master of my fate;
I am the captain of my soul.

William Ernest Henley

Whistling to keep up courage is good practice for whistling.

Henry Hoskins

Bravery

Perfect courage means doing unwitnessed what we would be capable of with the world looking on.

François de La Rochefoucauld

Keep your fears to yourself, but share your courage with others.

Robert Louis Stevenson

See also ACTION, CONFIDENCE

Business

Leaders are people who do the right things. Managers are people who do things right . . . a profound difference.

Warren Bennis

The chief business of the American people is business.

Calvin Coolidge

There are very honest people who do not think they have had a bargain unless they have cheated a merchant.

Anatole France

America can no more survive and grow without big business than it can survive and grow without small business.

Benjamin Franklin

Only the paranoid survive.

Andrew S. Grove

Whatever is not nailed down is mine. Whatever I can pry loose is not nailed down.

Collis P. Huntington

If we did not have such a thing as an airplane today we would probably create something like NASA to make one.

H. Ross Perot

One third of the people in the U.S. promote while the other two thirds provide.

Will Rogers

There is hardly anything in the world that some man cannot make a little worse and sell a little cheaper.

John Ruskin

Business

There is something about a bureaucrat that does not like a poem.

Gore Vidal

A corporation cannot blush.

Henry Collins Walsh

Being good in business is the most fascinating kind of art.

Andy Warhol

See also COMPUTERS, DEBT, MONEY, TAXES

Cats

Those who'll play with cats must expect to be scratched.

Miguel de Cervantes

Cats seem to go on the principle that it never does any harm to ask for what you want.

Joseph Krutch

No matter how much cats fight, there always seem to be plenty of kittens.

Abraham Lincoln

When I play with my cat, who knows but that
she regards me more as a plaything than I do her.

Michel de Montaigne

See also ANIMALS, DOGS

Celebrity

A celebrity is a person who works hard all his life
to become well-known, then wears dark glasses to
avoid being recognized.

Fred Allen

When once a man has made celebrity necessary
to his happiness, he has put it in the power of the
weakest and most timorous malignity, if not to
take away his satisfaction, at least to withhold it.

Samuel Johnson

The great are great only because we are on our
knees.

Pierre Joseph Proudhon

Celebrity sells dearly what we think she gives.

Souvestre

Celebrity

Censure is the tax a man pays to the public for being eminent.

Jonathan Swift

See also FAME, SUCCESS

Change

Not everything that is faced can be changed, but nothing can be changed until it is faced.

James Baldwin

It's hard for me to get used to these changing times; I can remember when the air was clean and sex was dirty.

George Burns

Nothing endures but change.

Heraclitus

Change is not progress.

H. L. Mencken

Things don't change, but, by and by, our wishes change.

Marcel Proust

The reasonable man adapts himself to the world; the unreasonable one persists in trying to adapt the world to himself. Therefore, all progress depends on the unreasonable man.

George Bernard Shaw

The art of progress is to preserve order amid change and to preserve change amid order.

Alfred North Whitehead

If you want to make enemies, try to change something.

Woodrow Wilson

Character

For the good man to realize that it is better to be whole than good is to enter on a straight and narrow path compared to which his previous rectitude was flowery license.

Anonymous

Character builds slowly, but it can be torn down again with incredible swiftness.

Faith Baldwin

Character

Everyone is necessarily the hero of his own life story.

John Barth

Blessed is he who has reached the point of no return and knows it, for he shall enjoy living.

William Bennett

Nothing really sets human nature free but self-control.

Paul Bottome

When a man's fight begins within himself, he is worth something.

Robert Browning

All that we are is the result of what we have thought. The mind is everything. What we think, we become.

Buddha

When you look into a mirror, you do not see your reflection; your reflection sees you.

Daedalus

Do not say things. What you are stands over you the while and thunders so that I cannot hear what you say to the contrary.

Ralph Waldo Emerson

It is better to be hated for what you are than loved for what you are not.

André Gide

What is character but the determination of incident? What is incident but the illustration of character?

Henry James

Until we lose ourselves, there is no hope of finding ourselves.

Henry Miller

When you make a world tolerable for yourself, you make a world tolerable for others.

Anaïs Nin

Better keep yourself clean and bright; you are the window through which you must see the world.

George Bernard Shaw

Character

Acquit me, or do not acquit me, but be sure that I shall not alter my way of life, no, not if I have to die for it many times.

Socrates

The most important thing is to be whatever you are without shame.

Rod Steiger

The universe seems bankrupt as soon as we begin to discuss the character of individuals.

Henry David Thoreau

See also BEHAVIOR, CONVICTIONS, INDIVIDUALISM, PATIENCE

Charm

The greatest mistake is trying to be more agreeable than you can be.

Walter Bagehot

If you have it [charm], you don't need to have anything else, and if you don't have it, it doesn't much matter what else you have.

Sir James M. Barrie

Nothing is so old as a dilapidated charm.

Emily Dickinson

Once the charmer is aware of a mannerism or characteristic that others find charming, it ceases to be a mannerism and becomes an affectation. And good Lord, there is nothing less charming than affectations!

Rex Harrison

Chastity

Give me chastity and continency, but not yet.

St. Augustine

Of all sexual aberrations, perhaps the most peculiar is chastity.

Rémy de Gourmont

Chastity: the most unnatural of sexual perversions.

Aldous Huxley

Marriage has many pains, but celibacy has no pleasures.

Samuel Johnson

Chastity

The resistance of a woman is not always proof of her virtue, but more frequently of her experience.

Ninon de L'Enclos

An unattempted woman cannot boast of her chastity.

Michel de Montaigne

Chaste is she whom no one has asked.

Ovid

See also SEX

Children

Children sweeten labors, but they make misfortune more bitter.

Anonymous

Even a minor event in the life of a child is an event of that child's world and th us a world event.

Gaston Bachelard

What is an adult? A child blown up by age.

Simone de Beauvoir

Never lend your car to anyone to whom you have given birth.

Erma Bombeck

The thorns which I have reaped are of the tree I planted.

Lord Byron

Something you consider bad may bring out your child's talents; something you consider good may stifle them.

François René de Chateaubriand

Every boy in his heart would rather steal second base than an automobile.

Tom Clarke

Always be nice to your children because they are the ones who will choose your rest home.

Phyllis Diller

The mother of the year should be a sterilized woman with two children.

Paul Ehrlich

Children

We find delight in the beauty and happiness of children that makes the heart too big for the body.

Ralph Waldo Emerson

Every child is born a genius.

Robert Fuller

We can't form our children on our own concepts; we must take them and love them as God gives them to us.

Johann Wolfgang von Goethe

The young man knows the rules, but the old man knows the exceptions.

Oliver Wendell Holmes

Allow children to be happy in their own way, for what better way will they ever find?

Samuel Johnson

Children are a great comfort in your old age and they help you to reach it faster, too.

Lionel Kaufman

All God's children are not beautiful; most of God's children are, in fact, barely presentable.

Fran Lebowitz

Our children will hate us too, y' know.

Jack Lemmon

Posterity is the patriotic name for grandchildren.

Art Linkletter

I love children, especially when they cry. Then someone takes them away.

Nancy Mitford

The maturity of man: to have reacquired the seriousness he had as a child at play.

Friedrich Wilhelm Nietzsche

If you bungle raising your children I don't think whatever else you do matters.

Jacqueline Kennedy Onassis

The best way to keep children at home is to make the atmosphere pleasant and let the air out of the tires.

Dorothy Parker

Children

Before I got married, I had six theories about bringing up children; now I have six children and no theories.

Lord Rochester

The fundamental defect of fathers is that they want their children to be a credit to them.

Bertrand Russell

Adults are obsolete children.

Dr. Seuss

How sharper than a serpent's tooth it is
To have a thankless child.

William Shakespeare: King Lear

The more you love your children, the more care you should take to neglect them occasionally. The web of affection can be drawn too tight.

David Sutton

Permissiveness is the principle of treating children as if they were adults and the tactic of making sure they never reach that stage.

Thomas Szasz

Children begin by loving their parents; as they grow older they judge them; sometimes they forgive them.

Oscar Wilde

See also ADOLESCENCE, AGE, FAMILY, PARENTS, YOUTH

Christianity

Christianity is so full of fraud that any honest man should renounce the whole shebang and espouse atheism instead.

Paul Blanchard

You don't have to be perfect to be Christ. All you have to do is stick your neck out and say the system sucks. They'll find a way of nailing you to the cross.

Eric Burdon

If Jesus Christ were to come today, people would not even crucify him. They would ask him to dinner and hear what he had to say and make fun of it.

Thomas Carlyle

Christianity

Christianity is completed Judaism, or it is nothing.

Benjamin Disraeli

Christ died for our sins. Dare we make his martyrdom meaningless by not committing them?

Jules Feiffer

Christians never were meant to be respectable.

Harry Emerson Fosdick

The good news is that Jesus is coming back. The bad news is that He's really pissed off.

Bob Hope

If Christian nations were nations of Christians, there would be no wars.

Soame Jenyns

Christendom has done away with Christianity without being quite aware of it.

Søren Kierkegaard

To the frivolous, Christianity is certainly not glad tidings, for it wishes first of all to make them serious.

Søren Kierkegaard

No kingdom has ever had as many civil wars as the kingdom of Christ.

Baron de Montesquieu

See also AFTERLIFE, BELIEFS, BIBLE, GOD, HELL, RELIGION

Civilization

A new vision of development is emerging. Development is becoming a people-centered process, whose ultimate goal must be the improvement of the human condition.

Boutros Boutros-Ghali

Perfection of means and confusion of ends seem to characterize our age.

Albert Einstein

Civilization has spread until television and jet bombers can be heard everywhere.

Herbert Prochnow

Civilization is, after all, but a coat of paint that washes away when the rain falls.

Auguste Rodin

Civilization

The universal regard for money is one hopeful fact in our civilization.

George Bernard Shaw

Civilization is progress from an indefinite incoherent homogeneity toward a definite coherent heterogeneity.

Herbert Spencer

Civilization is a movement and not a condition. A voyage and not a harbor.

Arnold Toynbee

Human history becomes more and more a race between education and catastrophe.

H. G. Wells

See also MAN

Committees

To kill time, a committee meeting is the perfect weapon.

Fred Allen

Committee: a group of men who keep minutes and waste hours.

Anonymous

Committee: a group of the unfit appointed by the unwilling to do the unnecessary.

Stewart Harrol

A committee is a thing which takes a week to do what one good man can do in an hour.

Elbert Hubbard

No committee could ever come up with anything as revolutionary as a camel—anything as practical and as perfectly designed to perform effectively under such difficult conditions.

Laurence J. Peter

Nothing is ever accomplished by a committee unless it consists of three members, one of whom happens to be sick and the other absent.

Hendrik Willem Van Loon

Committees

A camel looks like a horse that was planned by a committee.

Vogue *magazine*

See also DEMOCRACY, GOVERNMENT

Computers

Someday, computers may not only be able to beat human beings at chess, but also at tennis and ice hockey and volleyball. Someday, computers may be able to marry Brooke Shields.

Christopher Buckley

Enthusiasm for a medium that keeps you away from human beings strikes me as worrying.

Ian Hislop

The new electronic interdependence recreates the world in the image of a global village.

Marshall McLuhan

I have become seriously intimidated by the need of my computer to win on every occasion. I now approach each Scrabble game with an irrational fear. Gary Kasparov has my sympathy.

Sir Roger Penrose

If computers can cheat, then they can love, hate and conspire.

Sir Roger Penrose

Intelligence cannot be present without understanding. No computer has any awareness of what it does.

Sir Roger Penrose

Computers make it easier to do a lot of things, but most of the things they make it easier to do don't need to be done.

Andy Rooney

A computer doesn't charge for overtime and doesn't get health care benefits.

Adam Smith

Computers have enabled unprecedented realism in special effects. Maybe someday faster and cheaper computers will make it possible to do away with actors. We'll just pay a licensing fee for the Sly or Arnold software.

George Willis

See also BUSINESS

Conceit

Conceit is God's gift to little men.

Bruce Barton

He was like a cock who thought the sun had risen to hear him crow.

George Eliot

I've never any pity for conceited people, because I think they carry their comfort about with them.

George Eliot

When a man is wrapped up in himself, he makes a pretty small package.

John Ruskin

Conceit is incompatible with understanding.

Leo Tolstoy

See also BEAUTY, EGO, VANITY

Confidence

When you're as great as I am, it's hard to be humble.

Mohammed Ali

Confidence is simply the fervent assured feeling you have before you fall flat on your face.

C. Bruder

Confidence: the feeling that makes one believe a man, even when one knows that one would lie in his place.

H. L. Mencken

If you're knocked down, you can't lose your guts. You need to play with supreme confidence or else you'll lose again, and then losing becomes a habit.

Joe Paterno

Don't give up. Don't lose hope. Don't sell out.

Christopher Reeve

All you need in this life is ignorance and confidence and then success is sure.

Mark Twain

Confidence

You have noticed that the less I know about a subject, the more confidence I have, and the more light I throw on it.

Mark Twain

See also ACTION, BRAVERY, SUCCESS

Conformity

Force, violence, pressure, or compulsion with a view to conformity are both uncivilized and undemocratic.

Mahatma Gandhi

Every society honors its live conformists and its dead troublemakers.

Michael McLaughlin

There is no conversation more boring than where everybody agrees.

Michel de Montaigne

Lots of times, you have to pretend to join a parade in which you are really not interested in order to get where you are going.

Christopher Morley

Comedy is the last refuge of the nonconformist mind.

Gilbert Seldes

See also INDIVIDUALISM, ORIGINALITY

Conscience

Conscience is a cur that will let you get past it but that you cannot keep from barking.

Anonymous

The unknown is an ocean. What is conscience? The compass of the unknown.

Joseph Cook

Men of character are the conscience of the society to which they belong.

Ralph Waldo Emerson

Conscience is the inner voice that warns us somebody may be looking.

H. L. Mencken

Conscience and cowardice are really the same things.

Oscar Wilde

See also MORALITY

Conservative

Conservative: a statesman who is enamored of existing evils, as distinguished from the Liberal who wishes to replace them with others.

Ambrose Bierce

The world is burdened with young fogies. They are men who look young, act young and everlastingly harp on the fact that they are young, but who invariably act with a degree of caution that would be excessive in their grandfathers. They are the curse of the world.

Robertson Davies

Men are conservatives when they are least vigorous, or when they are most luxurious. They are conservatives after dinner.

Ralph Waldo Emerson

A conservative is a man who will not look at the new moon, out of respect for that "ancient institution," the old one.

Douglas Jerrold

Men who are orthodox when they are young are in danger of being middle-aged all their lives.

Walter Lippmann

We look like Republicans, and think like conservatives, but we drive a lot faster and keep vibrators and baby oil and a video camera behind the stack of sweaters on the bedroom closet shelf.

P. J. O'Rourke

A conservative is a man with two perfectly good legs who has never learned to walk.

Franklin D. Roosevelt

Loyalty to petrified opinion never yet broke a chain or freed a human soul.

Mark Twain

No man can be a conservative until he has something to lose.

James Paul Warburg

To be conservative requires no brains whatsoever. Cabbages, cows and conifers are conservative and

Conservative

are so stupid they don't even know it. All that is basically required is acceptance of what exists.

Colin Welch

A conservative is a man who just sits and thinks, mostly sits.

Woodrow Wilson

See also LIBERAL, POLITICS

Contentment

He is a wise man who does not grieve for the things which he has not, but rejoices for those which he has.

Epictetus

If wrinkles must be written upon our brows, let them not be written upon the heart. The spirit should not grow old.

James Garfield

Sweet are the thoughts that savor of content;
The quiet mind is richer than a crown.

Robert Greene

Winter is in my head, but spring is in my heart.

Victor Hugo

Before we set our hearts too much upon anything, let us examine how happy they are who
already possess it.

François de La Rochefoucauld

See also PEACE

Conversation

There are things which it is not only impossible
to discuss intelligently, but which it is not even
intelligent to discuss.

Feodor Dostoyevsky

Better to remain silent and to be thought a fool
than to speak out and remove all doubt.

Abraham Lincoln

A good listener is not only popular everywhere,
but after a while, he knows something.

Wilson Mizner

Conversation

The real art of conversation is not only to say the right thing in the right place but to leave unsaid the wrong thing at the tempting moment.

Dorothy Nevill

Wise men talk because they have something to say; fools, because they have to say something.

Plato

He has occasional flashes of silence that make his conversation perfectly delightful.

Sydney Smith

Whenever one has anything unpleasant to say, one should always be quite candid.

Oscar Wilde

See also SILENCE, TALK

Convictions

Strong beliefs win strong men, and then make them stronger.

Walter Bagehot

Neutral men are the devil's allies.

E. Chapin

So long as I am acting from duty and conviction,
I am indifferent to taunts and jeers; I think they
will probably do me more good than harm.

Winston Churchill

At eighteen our convictions are hills from which
we look; at forty-five they are caves in which we
hide.

F. Scott Fitzgerald

One needs to be slow to form convictions, but
once formed, they must be defended against the
heaviest odds.

Mahatma Gandhi

A very popular error—having the courage of
one's convictions; rather, it is a matter of having
the courage for an attack upon one's convictions.

Friedrich Wilhelm Nietzsche

Convictions are more dangerous enemies of truth
than lies.

Friedrich Wilhelm Nietzsche

See also BELIEFS, CHARACTER, OPINIONS,
PREJUDICE

Creativity

To a writer or painter, creation is the repayment of a debt. He suffers from a perpetual bad conscience until he has done this.

Gerald Brenan

The creative impulses of man are always at war with the possessive impulses.

Van Wyck Brooks

You've got to create a dream. You've got to uphold the dream. If you can't, then bugger it. Go back to the factory, or go back to the desk.

Eric Burdon

All men are creative, but few are artists.

Paul Goodman

Some men see things as they are and say "why?" I dream things that never were and say, "Why not?"

John F. Kennedy

True creativity often starts where language ends.

Arthur Koestler

Creativity can solve almost any problem. The creative act, the defeat of habit by originality overcomes everything.

George Lois

A creator needs only one enthusiast to justify him.

Man Ray

See also THE ARTS, MUSIC, ORIGINALITY, WORDS

Crime

When I see the ten most-wanted list, I always have this thought: if we'd made them feel wanted earlier, they wouldn't be wanted now.

Eddie Cantor

Capital punishment is as fundamentally wrong as a cure for crime as charity is wrong as a cure for poverty.

Henry Ford

It is worse than a crime; it is a blunder.

Joseph Fouché

Crime

Every once in a while, some feller without a single bad habit gets caught.

Kin (Frank McKinney) Hubbard

Many commit the same crime with very different results. One bears a cross for his crime, the other a crown.

Bertrand de Juvenal

A criminal is a person with predatory instincts who has not sufficient capital to form a corporation.

Howard Scott

Most people fancy themselves innocent of those crimes of which they cannot be convicted.

Seneca

If England treats her criminals the way she has treated me, she doesn't deserve to have any.

Oscar Wilde

See also EVIL, JUSTICE, LAWS, VICE

Criticism

They couldn't find the artist, so they hung the picture.

Anonymous

It was one of those plays in which the actors, unfortunately, enunciated very clearly.

Robert Benchley

The covers of this book are too far apart.

Ambrose Bierce

There is no man so friendless but that he can find a friend sincere enough to tell him disagreeable truths.

Edward Bulwer-Lytton

Show me a man who insists that he welcomes criticism if only it is constructive, and I will show you a man who does not want any criticism at all.

Harold L. Ickes

Criticism comes easier than craftsmanship.

Zeuxis

See also ADVICE, DEPRECATION, TRUTH

Death

It's not that I'm afraid to die. I just don't want to be there when it happens.

Woody Allen

It is good to die before one has done anything deserving death.

Anaxandrides

To die will be an awfully big adventure.

Sir James M. Barrie

Until death, it is all life.

Miguel de Cervantes

All I desire for my own funeral is not to be buried alive.

G. K. Chesterton

Worldly faces never look so worldly as at a funeral.

T. S. Eliot

Death keeps no calendar.

Thomas Fuller

No man should be afraid to die who hath understood what it is to live.

Thomas Fuller

You can't tell how good it is to be alive till you're facing death because you don't live till then.

John Galsworthy

We sometimes congratulate ourselves at the moment of waking from a troubled dream; it may be so the moment after death.

Nathaniel Hawthorne

Our repugnance of death increases in proportion to our consciousness of having lived in vain.

William Hazlitt

There's one thing that keeps surprising you about stormy old friends after they die—their silence.

Ben Hecht

To save a man's life against his will is the same as killing him.

Horace

It matters not how a man dies, but how he lives.

Samuel Johnson

Death

To the psychiatrist an old man who cannot bid
farewell to life appears as feeble and sickly as a
young man who is unable to embrace it.

Carl Jung

If a man hasn't discovered something that he will
die for, he isn't fit to live.

Martin Luther King, Jr.

If some persons died, and others did not die,
death would indeed be a terrible affliction.

Jean de La Bruyère

We must laugh before we are happy, for fear we
die before we laugh at all.

Jean de La Bruyère

Some men are more missed than lamented, when
they die. Others are deeply mourned but scarcely
missed.

François de La Rochefoucauld

A man's dying is more the survivors' affair than
his own.

Thomas Mann

If death did not exist, it would be necessary to invent it.

J. Milhaud

Into the darkness they go, the wise and the lovely.

Edna St. Vincent Millay

It is not death that alarms me, but dying.

Michel de Montaigne

The most frightful idea that has ever corroded human nature—the idea of eternal punishment.

John Morley

I am going to seek a grand perhaps . . .

François Rabelais

To die is easy when we are in perfect health. On a fine spring morning, out of doors, mind and body sound and exhilarated, it would be nothing to lie down on the turf and pass away.

Mark Rutherford

After your death you will be what you were before your birth.

Arthur Schopenhauer

Death

Every day is a little life; every waking and rising a little birth, every fresh morning a little youth, every going to rest and sleep a little death.

Arthur Schopenhauer

Moderate lamentation is the right of the dead, excessive grief the enemy to the living.

William Shakespeare: All's Well That Ends Well

But my troth, I care not, a man can die but once. We owe God a death.

William Shakespeare: Henry IV

Nothing is truer in a sense than a funeral oration. It tells precisely what the dead man should have been.

J. Vaperean

While I thought that I was learning how to live, I have been learning how to die.

Leonardo da Vinci

One may live as a conqueror, a king, or a magistrate, but he must die as a man.

Daniel Webster

I am dying beyond my means.

Oscar Wilde

See also AFTERLIFE, LIFE, YOUTH

Debt

If I had the privilege of making the Eleventh commandment it would be this—Owe no man.

Josh Billings

Never run into debt, not if you can find anything else to run into.

Josh Billings

We can only pay our debt to the past by putting the future in debt to ourselves.

John Buchan

Blessed are the young for they shall inherit the national debt.

Herbert Hoover

Creditors have better memories than debtors.

James Howell

Debt

Debt shortens life.

Joseph Joubert

Debt is the fatal disease of republics, the first thing and the mightiest to undermine government and corrupt the people.

Wendell Phillips

Some people use one half their ingenuity to get into debt, and the other half to avoid paying it.

George Prentice

See also BUSINESS, MONEY, POVERTY, TAXES

Deception

It is in the ability to deceive oneself that the greatest talent is shown.

Anatole France

We are never deceived. We deceive ourselves.

Johann Wolfgang von Goethe

Deceive not thy physician, confessor, nor lawyer.

George Herbert

It is a double pleasure to deceive the deceiver.

Jean de La Fontaine

It is true that you may fool all the people some of
the time; you can even fool some of the people
all the time; but you cannot fool all of the people
all the time.

Abraham Lincoln

Wooden-headedness, the source of self-deception,
is a factor that plays a remarkably large role in
government . . . It is acting according to wish
while not allowing oneself to be deflected by the
facts.

Barbara Tuchman

See also HYPOCRISY, LYING, SINCERITY

Definitions

A definition is the enclosing of a wilderness of
ideas within a wall of words.

Samuel Butler

I had rather feel compunction than understand
the meaning of it.

Thomas à Kempis

Definitions

In the animal kingdom, the rule is, eat or be eaten; in the human kingdom, define or be defined.

Thomas Szasz

It is almost impossible to state what one in fact believes because it is almost impossible to hold a belief and to define it at the same time.

William Carlos Williams

Democracy

Democracy means government by discussion, but it is only effective if you can stop people talking.

Clement Atlee

The ship of democracy which has weathered many storms may sink through the mutiny of those aboard.

Grover Cleveland

Democracy consists of choosing your dictators after they've told you what you think it is you want to hear.

Arnold Coven

Democracy is based upon the conviction that there are extraordinary possibilities in ordinary people.

Harry Emerson Fosdick

The job of a citizen is to keep his mouth open.

Günter Grass

Democracy gives every man the right to be his own oppressor.

John Lowell

Democracy is the art of running the circus from the monkey cage.

H. L. Mencken

Democracy substitutes election by the incompetent many for appointment by the corrupt few.

George Bernard Shaw

It's not the voting that's democracy; it's the counting.

Tom Stoppard

In Switzerland, they had brotherly love, five hundred years of democracy, and peace, and what did they produce: the cuckoo clock.

Orson Welles

Democracy

Democracy means simply the bludgeoning of the people by the people for the people.

Oscar Wilde

I believe in democracy because it releases the energies of every human being.

Woodrow Wilson

See also COMMITTEES, GOVERNMENT

Deprecation

Those who have free seats at a play hiss first.

Anonymous

They condemn what they do not understand.

Cicero

Don't abuse your friends and expect them to consider it criticism.

Edgar Watson Howe

We would rather speak ill of ourselves than not talk of ourselves at all.

François de La Rochefoucauld

See also BLAME, CRITICISM, FORGIVING

Desire and Longing

He who desires, but acts not, breeds pestilence.

William Blake

We grow weary of those things (and perhaps soonest) which we most desire.

Samuel Butler

The animal needing something knows how much it needs; the man does not.

Democritus

Much will have more.

Ralph Waldo Emerson

The average man who does not know what to do with his life wants another one which will last forever.

Anatole France

Some say the world will end in fire,
Some say in ice.
From what I've tasted of desire
I hold with those who favor fire.

Robert Frost

Desire and Longing

Desire is half of life; indifference is half of death.

Khalil Gibran

Every seed is a longing.

Khalil Gibran

Life contains but two tragedies. One is not to get your heart's desire; the other is to get it.

Socrates

An aspiration is a joy forever, a possession as solid as a landed estate.

Adlai Stevenson

Desperation

When we are flat on our back, there is no way to look but up.

Roger Babson

Never despair. But if you do, work on in despair.

D. Burke

Facing it, always facing it, that's the way to get through. Face it.

Joseph Conrad

Despair is the damp of hell as joy is the serenity of heaven.

John Donne

When a man has reached a condition in which he believes that a thing must happen because he does not wish it, and that what he wishes to happen can never be, this is really the state called despair.

Arthur Schopenhauer

I must lose myself in action lest I wither in despair.

Alfred Lord Tennyson

What is called resignation is confirmed desperation.

Henry David Thoreau

See also ALCOHOL, EMPTINESS, LONELINESS

Diet

He dreamed he was eating shredded wheat and woke up to find the mattress half gone.

Fred Allen

Diet

Tell me what you eat, and I'll tell you what you are.

Anthelme Brillat-Savarin

As a child, my family's meal consisted of two choices: take it or leave it.

Buddy Hackett

I told my doctor I got very tired when I go on a diet, so he gave me pep pills. Know what happened? I ate faster.

Joe E. Lewis

The chief excitement in a woman's life is spotting women who are fatter than she is.

Helen Rowland

See also FOOD, HEALTH

Diplomats

I have discovered the art of foiling diplomats. I speak the truth, and they never believe me.

Camillo Benso Conte di Cavour

Direction

An appeaser is one who feeds a crocodile hoping it will eat him last.

Winston Churchill

A diplomat is a man who always remembers a woman's birthday but never remembers her age.

Robert Frost

A diplomat is one who can cut his neighbor's throat without his neighbor noticing it.

Carlos P. Romulo

Diplomacy is the art of letting someone have your way.

Daniele Varè

See also GOVERNMENT

Direction

The dodo flies backward because he doesn't care to see where he's going, but wants to see where he's been.

Fred Allen

Direction

If you cry, "Forward," you must be sure to make clear the direction in which to go. Don't you see that if you fail to do that and simply call out the word to a monk and a revolutionary, they will go in precisely opposite directions.

Anton Chekhov

The person who makes a success of living is the one who sees his goal steadily and aims for it unswervingly. That is dedication.

Cecil B. DeMille

Men, like nails, lose their usefulness when they lose direction and begin to bend.

Walter Landor

Disappointment

The disappointment of manhood succeeds the delusion of youth.

Benjamin Disraeli

How disappointment tracks the steps of hope.

L. London

"Blessed is the man who expects nothing, for he shall never be disappointed" was the ninth beatitude which a man of wit . . . added to the eighth.

Alexander Pope

Blessed be he who expects nothing, for he shall never be disappointed.

Jonathan Swift

For of all sad words of tongue or pen,
The saddest are these: "It might have been!"

John Greenleaf Whittier

Disease

Cure the disease and kill the patient.

Francis Bacon

Illness is a convent which has its rule, its austerity, its silences and its inspirations.

Albert Camus

It takes a wise doctor to know when not to prescribe.

Baltasar Gracián

Disease

How sickness enlarges the dimensions of man's self to himself.

Charles Lamb

Optimistic lies have such immense therapeutic value that a doctor who cannot tell them convincingly has mistaken his profession.

George Bernard Shaw

Formerly, when religion was strong and science weak, men mistook magic for medicine; now, when science is strong and religion weak, men mistake medicine for magic.

Thomas Szasz

See also DOCTORS, HEALTH

Divorce

Marriage is grounds for divorce.

Anonymous

It wasn't exactly a divorce—I was traded.

Tim Conway

Love the quest; marriage the conquest; divorce the inquest.

Helen Rowland

It's well to be off with the old woman before you're on with the new.

George Bernard Shaw

See also *ALIMONY, MARRIAGE*

Doctors

A doctor, like anyone else who has to deal with human beings, each of them unique, cannot be a scientist; he is either, like the surgeon, a craftsman, or, like the physician and the psychologist, an artist.

W. H. Auden

Never go to a doctor whose office plants have died.

Erma Bombeck

The threat of a neglected cold is for doctors what the threat of purgatory is for priests: a gold mine.

Nicolas Chamfort

Doctors

God heals, and the doctor takes the fee.

Benjamin Franklin

Whenever a doctor cannot do good, he must be kept from doing harm.

Hippocrates

Doctors are men who prescribe medicines of which they know little to cure diseases of which they know less in human beings of whom they know nothing.

Voltaire

See also DISEASE, HEALTH

Dogs

The dog was created especially for children. He is the god of frolic.

Henry Ward Beecher

A dog is the only thing on this earth that loves you more than he loves himself.

Josh Billings

If you pick up a starving dog and make him prosperous, he will not bite you. That is the principal difference between a dog and a man.

Mark Twain

They say a reasonable amount o' fleas is good fer a dog—keeps him from broodin' over *bein'* a dog.

Edward Westcott

See also ANIMALS, CATS

Drama

One of my chief regrets during my years in the theater is that I couldn't sit in the audience and watch me.

John Barrymore

If you want something from an audience, you give blood to their fantasies. It's the ultimate hustle.

Marlon Brando

In all ages the drama, through its portrayal of the acting and suffering spirit of man, has been more

Drama

closely allied than any other art to his deeper thoughts concerning his nature and his destiny.

Ludwig Lewisohn

As long as more people will pay admission to a theater to see a naked body than to see a naked brain, the drama will languish.

George Bernard Shaw

The world is a comedy to those who think and a tragedy to those who feel.

Horace Walpole

See also ACTING, HOLLYWOOD, TELEVISION

Dreams

Lift up your eyes upon
This day breaking for you.
Give birth again
To the dream.

Maya Angelou

The inquiry into a dream is another dream.

Lord Halifax

I am so unhappy at the present time that in my dreams I am indescribably happy.

Søren Kierkegaard

If people would recount their dreams truthfully, one might divine character more correctly from dreams than from faces.

Georg Christoph Lichtenberg

The republic is a dream,
Nothing happens unless first a dream.

Carl Sandburg

See also HOPE, OPTIMISM

Education

Nothing in education is so astonishing as the amount of ignorance it accumulates in the form of inert facts.

Henry Adams

Crafty men condemn studies; simple men admire them, and wise men use them.

Francis Bacon

Education

The eagle never lost so much time as when he submitted to learn of the crow.

William Blake

If you think education is expensive, try ignorance.

Derek Bok

It is better to speak wisdom foolishly like the saints than to speak folly wisely like the deans.

G. K. Chesterton

Education is a state-controlled manufactory of echoes.

Norman Douglas

When a subject becomes totally obsolete, we make it a required course.

Peter Drucker

If a man's education is finished, he is finished.

Edward Filene

A learned blockhead is a greater blockhead than an ignorant one.

Benjamin Franklin

Mistakes are their own instructors.

Horace

Stand firm in your refusal to remain conscious during algebra. In real life, I assure you there is no such thing as algebra.

Fran Lebowitz

Our American professors like their literature clear and cold and pure and very dead.

Sinclair Lewis

It now costs more to amuse a child than it once did to educate his father.

Vaughan Monroe

We receive three educations, one from our parents, one from our schoolmaster, and one from the world. The third contradicts all that the first two teach us.

Baron de Montesquieu

An educated man may earn more, but it takes him about twenty years after graduating to get educated.

Herbert Prochnow

Education

A man who has never gone to school may steal from a freight car, but if he has had a university education, he may steal from the whole railroad.

Theodore Roosevelt

An education obtained with money is worse than no education obtained at all.

Socrates

Soap and education are not as sudden as a massacre, but they are more deadly in the long run.

Mark Twain

See also AUTHORS, BOOKS, IGNORANCE, LEARNING, READING, WORDS

Ego

It's too bad I'm not as wonderful a person as people say I am, because the world could use a few people like that.

Alan Alda

The source of our actions resides in an unconscious propensity to regard ourselves as the center, the cause, and the conclusion of time.

E. M. Cioran

He that falls in love with himself will have no rivals.

Benjamin Franklin

You have no idea of what a poor opinion I have of myself, and how little I deserve it.

Sir William S. Gilbert

There are two sides to every question: my side and the wrong side.

Oscar Levant

How glorious it is and how pointed to be an exception.

Alfred de Musset

Never to talk about oneself is a very refined form of hypocrisy.

Friedrich Wilhelm Nietzsche

The golden fleece of self-love is proof against cudgel blows but not against pinpricks.

Friedrich Wilhelm Nietzsche

It astounds us to come upon other egoists, as though we alone have the right to be selfish and to be filled with eagerness to live.

Jules Renard

Ego

To love oneself is the beginning of a life-long
romance.

Oscar Wilde

See also CONCEIT, SELF, VANITY

Emptiness

In the small hours when the acrid stench of existence rises like sewer gas from every thing created, the emptiness of life seems more terrible than
its misery.

Cyril Connolly

When my cup is empty, I resign myself to its
emptiness, but when it is half full, I resent its half-
fullness.

Khalil Gibran

Our greatest pretenses are built up not to hide the
evil and the ugly in us, but our emptiness.

Eric Hoffer

See also ALCOHOL, DESPERATION, LONELINESS

Enemies

It is difficult to say who does you the most mischief: enemies with the worst intentions or friends with the best intentions.

Edward Bulwer-Lytton

It is not necessary to have enemies if you go out of your way to make friends.

F. Dane

You will be quite friendly with your enemy when you both die.

Khalil Gibran

Instead of loving your enemies treat your friends a little better.

Edgar Watson Howe

If you have no enemies, you are apt to be in the same predicament in regard to friends.

Elbert Hubbard

Friends may come and go, but enemies accumulate.

T. Jones

Enemies

We have met the enemy, and it is us.

Walt Kelly

A friend is one who has the same enemies you have.

Abraham Lincoln

Scratch a love, and find a foe.

Dorothy Parker

To forgive our enemies their virtues, that is a greater miracle.

Voltaire

A man cannot be too careful in the choice of his enemies.

Oscar Wilde

Speak well of your enemies, sir. You made them.

Oscar Wilde

See also FRIENDSHIP, WAR

English

The English instinctively admire any man who has no talent and is modest about it.

James Agee

The British have a remarkable talent for keeping calm even when there is no crisis.

Franklin P. Jones

If you want to eat well in England, eat three breakfasts.

W. Somerset Maugham

The English have better sense than any other nation, and they are fools.

Klemens von Metternich

An Englishman thinks he is moral when he is only uncomfortable.

George Bernard Shaw

See also AMERICANS

Envy

Envy lurks at the bottom of the human heart like a viper in its hole.

Honoré de Balzac

The dullard's envy of brilliant men is always assuaged by the suspicion that they will come to a bad end.

Max Beerbohm

Envy

The silence of the envious is too noisy.

Khalil Gibran

Envy, among other ingredients, has a mixture of love of justice in it. We are more angry at undeserved than at deserved good fortune.

William Hazlitt

Envy is more implacable than hatred.

François de La Rochefoucauld

The gilded sheath of pity conceals the dagger of envy.

Friedrich Wilhelm Nietzsche

Compete, don't envy.

Arab proverb

Few of us can stand prosperity, another man's, I mean.

Mark Twain

Man will do many things to get himself loved; he will do all things to get himself envied.

Mark Twain

See also FEELINGS, JEALOUSY

Eternity

Eternal nothingness is fine if you happen to be dressed for it.

Woody Allen

Eternity is in love with the productions of time.

William Blake

Nothing is eternal, alas, except eternity.

Paul Fort

We do not know what to do with this short life, yet we want another which will be eternal.

Anatole France

The fact of having been born is a bad augury for immortality.

George Santayana

See also AFTERLIFE, BIBLE, GOD

Evil

You cannot have power for good without having power for evil too.

Anonymous

Evil

The Devil tempts men to be wicked that he may punish them for being so.

Samuel Butler

Wicked people sometimes perform good actions. I suppose they wish to see if this gives as great a feeling of pleasure as the virtuous claim for it.

Nicolas Chamfort

Evil comes at leisure like the disease; good comes in a hurry like the doctor.

G. K. Chesterton

The belief in a supernatural source of evil is not necessary; men alone are quite capable of every wickedness.

Joseph Conrad

Bad men do what good men only dream.

Gavin Ewart

Money is the fruit of evil, as often as the root of it.

Henry Fielding

The Devil himself is good when he is pleased.

Thomas Fuller

Evil is a fact, not to be explained away, but to be accepted; and accepted, not to be endured, but to be conquered.

John Haynes Holmes

Grief and disappointment give rise to anger, anger to envy, envy to malice, and malice to grief again, till the whole circle be completed.

David Hume

The lunatic's visions of horror are all drawn from the material of daily fact.

William James

Many might go to heaven with half the labor they go to hell.

Samuel Johnson

Few men are sufficiently discerning to appreciate the evil that they do.

François de La Rochefoucauld

There are bad people who would be less danger-ous if they had no good in them.

François de La Rochefoucauld

Evil

Man is almost always as wicked as his needs
require.

Giacomo Leopardi

Malicious men may die, but malice never.

Molière

Satan is inconsistent. He persuades a man not to
go to synagogue on a cold morning; yet when the
man does go, he follows him into it.

John Henry Cardinal Newman

Kill a man, and you are a murderer. Kill millions
of men, and you are a conqueror. Kill everyone,
and you are a god.

Jean Rostand

Man is the only animal who causes pain to others
with no other object than wanting to do so.

Arthur Schopenhauer

Even mother's milk nourishes murderers as well as
heroes.

George Bernard Shaw

I never wonder to see men wicked, but I often wonder to see them unashamed.

Jonathan Swift

Bad nature never lacks an instructor.

Publilius Syrus

Cruelty isn't softened by tears; it feeds on them.

Publilius Syrus

The wicked are always surprised to find that the good can be clever.

Marquis de Vauvenargues

We have neither the strength nor the opportunity to accomplish all the good and all the evil which we design.

Marquis de Vauvenargues

Between two evils, I always pick the one I never tried before.

Mae West

See also CRIME, GOODWILL, VICE, VIRTUE

Experience

Experience is a keen knife that hurts while it extracts the cataract that binds.

Anonymous

Experiences are savings which a miser puts aside; wisdom is an inheritance which a wastrel cannot exhaust.

Anonymous

Experience is a good teacher, but she sends in terrific bills.

Minna Antrim

Technology . . . the knack of so arranging the world that we don't have to experience it.

Max Frisch

One must pass through the circumference of time before arriving at the center of opportunity.

Baltasar Gracián

Some people have had nothing else but experience.

Don Herolde

Experience is not what happens to you. It is what you do with what happens to you.

Aldous Huxley

Experience is a hard teacher because she gives the test first, the lesson afterward.

Vernon Law

Everyone is perfectly willing to learn from unpleasant experiences, if only the damage of the first lesson could be repaired.

Georg Christoph Lichtenberg

Experience is the name men give to their follies or their sorrows.

Alfred de Musset

What does not destroy me makes me stronger.

Friedrich Wilhelm Nietzsche

Experience: a comb life gives you after you lose your hair.

Judith Stern

Better a monosyllabic life than a ragged and muttered one; let its report be short and round like a

Experience

rifle so that it may hear its own echo in the surrounding silence.

Henry David Thoreau

Experience is simply the name we give our mistakes.

Oscar Wilde

Failure

Failure is not the only punishment for laziness; there is also the success of others.

Anonymous

Nothing succeeds, they say, like success. And certainly, nothing fails like failure.

Anonymous

We are all failures, at least the best of us.

Anonymous

Ever tried. Ever failed. No matter. Try again. Fail again. Fail better.

Samuel Beckett

Nothing fails like success.

G. K. Chesterton

Notice the difference between what happens when a man says to himself, "I have failed three times" and what happens when he says "I am a failure."

S. I. Hayakawa

A failure is a man who has blundered but who is not able to cash in the experience.

Elbert Hubbard

Failure has no friends.

John F. Kennedy

You don't die in the U.S., you underachieve.

Jerzy Kozinski

There is no formula for success. But there is a formula for failure and that is trying to please everybody.

Man Ray

Men were born to succeed, not to fail.

Henry David Thoreau

See also SUCCESS

Faith

The success of any venture will be helped by prayer, even in the wrong denomination.

Anonymous

Faith: is belief without evidence to what is told by he who speaks without knowledge of things without parallel.

Ambrose Bierce

To believe only possibilities, is not faith, but mere Philosophy.

Sir Thomas Browne

The word "orthodoxy" not only no longer means not being right, it practically means being wrong.

G. K. Chesterton

I do not consider it an insult, but rather a compliment to be called an agnostic. I do not pretend to know where many ignorant men are sure—that is all that agnosticism means.

Clarence Darrow

I could prove God statistically.

George Gallup

The greatest act of faith is when man decides he
is not God.

Oliver Wendell Holmes

Every truth has two faces, every rule two surfaces,
every precept two applications.

Petrus Jacobus Joubert

Faith is under the left nipple.

Martin Luther

If a man have a strong faith he can indulge in the
luxury of skepticism.

Friedrich Wilhelm Nietzsche

Without faith, a man can do nothing; with it, all
things are possible.

William Osler

I love to pray at sunrise—before the world
becomes polluted with vanity and hatred.

The Koreiser Rabbi

Every miracle can be explained—after the event.
Not because the miracle is no miracle, but
because explanation is explanation.

Franz Rosenzweig

Faith

Complacency in the presence of miracles is like opening the door to your own tomb.

Rod Steiger

Martyrs create faith more than faith creates martyrs.

Miguel de Unamuno

See also BIBLE, GOD, RELIGION

Fame

If you would not be forgotten as soon as you are dead, either write things worth reading or do things worth writing.

Benjamin Franklin

A root is a flower that disdains fame.

Khalil Gibran

Popularity is a crime from the moment it is sought; it is only a virtue where men have it whether they will or no.

Lord Halifax

How many people live on the reputation of the reputation they might have made.

Oliver Wendell Holmes

Contempt of fame begets contempt of virtue.

Samuel Johnson

If fame is to come only after death, I am in no hurry for it.

Martial

It is better to be a has-been than a never-was.

Cecil Parkinson

Fame is so sweet that we love anything with which we connect it, even death.

Blaise Pascal

Why long for glory, which one despises as soon as one has it? But that is precisely what the ambitious man wants: having it in order to despise it.

Jean Rostand

Fame

Most celebrated men live in a condition of prostitution.

Charles-Augustin Sainte-Beuve

Wealth is like sea-water; the more we drink, the thirstier we become and the same is true of fame.

Arthur Schopenhauer

See also ACCOMPLISHMENT, ACHIEVEMENT, CELEBRITY, SUCCESS

Family

A friend who is near and dear may become as useless as a relative in time.

George Ade

The family is the nucleus of civilization.

Will Durant

He that has no fools, knaves, nor beggars in his family was begot by a flash of lightning.

Thomas Fuller

The family you come from isn't as important as the family you're going to have.

Ring Lardner

God gives us relations; thank God we can choose our friends.

Ethel Mumford

What was silent in the father speaks in the son, and often I have found the son the unveiled secret of the father.

Friedrich Wilhelm Nietzsche

Happy families are alike; every unhappy family is unhappy in its own way.

Leo Tolstoy

Why pay money to have your family tree traced? Go into politics when your opponents will do it for you.

Mark Twain

There are no illegitimate children, only illegitimate parents.

Leon Yankowich

See also ANCESTRY, CHILDREN, PARENTS

Fanaticism

A fanatic is incorruptible: if he kills for an idea, he can just as well get himself killed for one; in either case, tyrant or martyr, he is a monster.

E. M. Cioran

A fanatic is a man that does what he thinks the Lord would do if he knew the facts of the case.

Finley Peter Dunne

A fanatic is one who sticks to his guns, whether they're loaded or not.

Franklin P. Jones

Fanaticism consists in redoubling your efforts when you have forgotten your aim.

George Santayana

The weakness of the fanatic is that those whom he fights have a secret hold on him, and to this weakness, he and his group finally succumb.

Paul Tillich

The worst vice of the fanatic is his sincerity.

Oscar Wilde

Fashion

Fashion . . . a despot whom the wise ridicule and obey.

Ambrose Bierce

Dress is a very foolish thing, and yet, it is a very foolish thing for a man not to be well-dressed.

Lord Chesterfield

Fashion is gentility running away from vulgarity and afraid of being overtaken.

William Hazlitt

The fashion wears out more apparel than the man.

William Shakespeare: Much Ado About Nothing

A fashion is nothing but an induced epidemic.

George Bernard Shaw

Fashion is a form of ugliness so intolerable that we have to alter it every six months.

Oscar Wilde

Fashion

Fashion is that by which the fantastic becomes for the moment the universal.

Oscar Wilde

Woman's first duty in life is to her dressmaker. What the second duty is, no one has yet discovered.

Oscar Wilde

See also VANITY

Fate

Fortune is a God and rules men's lives.

Aeschylus

I do not believe in a fate that falls on men however they act, but I do believe in a fate that falls on men unless they act.

G. K. Chesterton

Lots of folks confuse management with destiny.

Kin (Frank McKinney) Hubbard

Successful men of action are not sufficiently self-observant to know exactly on what their success depends.

James Jacobs

The Moving Finger writes; and, having writ,
Moves on: nor all your Piety nor wit
Shall lure it back to cancel half a Line,
Nor all your Tears wash out a Word of it.

Omar Khayyám

See also LUCK, OPPORTUNITY

Fear

We fear something before we hate it. A child who
fears noises becomes a man that hates noise.

Cyril Connolly

Fear of becoming a has-been keeps some people
from becoming anything.

Eric Hoffer

A good scare is worth more to a man than good
advice.

Edgar Watson Howe

Fear of hypocrites and fools is the great plague of
thinking and writing.

Jules-Gabriel Janin

Fear

We have to realize that we are as deeply afraid to live and to love as we are to die.

Ronald David Laing

We mustn't fear daylight just because it almost always illuminates a miserable world.

René Magritte

The only thing we have to fear is fear itself.

Franklin D. Roosevelt

To conquer fear is the beginning of wisdom.

Bertrand Russell

Whoever is abandoned by hope has also been abandoned by fear; this is the meaning of the word "desperate."

Arthur Schopenhauer

To a man who is afraid, everything rustles.

Sophocles

Fear cannot be without hope nor hope without fear.

Baruch Spinoza

Quiet minds cannot be perplexed or frightened but go on in fortune or misfortune at their own private pace, like a clock in a thunderstorm.

Robert Louis Stevenson

See also FEELINGS

Feelings

Feelings are never true. They play with their mirrors.

Jean Baudrillard

Nothing is more injurious to the character and to the intellect than the suppression of generous emotion.

John Jay Chapman

If merely "feeling good" could decide, drunkenness would be the supremely valid human experience.

William James

Those who do not feel pain seldom think that it is felt.

Samuel Johnson

Feelings

It is harder to hide feelings we have than to feign those we lack.

François de La Rochefoucauld

We feel in one world. We think in another. Between the two, we can set up a series of references, but we cannot fill the gap.

Marcel Proust

No one can make you feel inferior without your consent.

Eleanor Roosevelt

I feel like the small boy who stubbed his toe; he was too old to cry, and it hurt too much to laugh.

Adlai Stevenson

There is always something ridiculous about the emotions of people whom one has ceased to love.

Oscar Wilde

See also ANGER, ENVY, FEAR, GRIEF, HAPPINESS, HATE, HOPE, JEALOUSLY, JOY, LOVE, SORROW

Films

The film is a machine for seeing more than meets the eye.

I. Barry

A film is a petrified garden of thought.

Jean Cocteau

A film is the world in an hour and a half.

Jean-Luc Godard

The cinema is truth twenty-four times a second.

Jean-Luc Godard

It's more than magnificent. It's mediocre.

Samuel Goldwyn

What we want is a story that starts with an earth-quake and works its way up to a climax.

Samuel Goldwyn

The cinema is not a slice of life. It's a piece of cake.

Alfred Hitchcock

Films

American motion pictures are written by the half-educated for the half-witted.

S. Irvine

Cinema should make you forget you're sitting in a theatre.

Roman Polanski

The cinema has no boundaries. It is a ribbon of dream.

Orson Welles

The trouble with a movie these days is that it is old before it is released. It is no accident that it comes in a can.

Orson Welles

The movies spoil us for life; nothing ever lives up to them.

Edmund White

A movie without sex would be like a candy bar without nuts.

Earl Wilson

See also ACTING, HOLLYWOOD, TALENT

Flattery

When a man is really important, the worst adviser he can have is a flatterer.

Anonymous

After a man is fifty you can fool him by saying he is smart, but you can't fool him by saying he is pretty.

Edgar Watson Howe

Just praise is a debt, but flattery is a present.

Samuel Johnson

We seek our happiness outside ourselves, and in the opinion of men who we know to be flatterers, insincere, unjust, full of envy, caprice, and prejudice. How absurd.

Jean de La Bruyère

Flattery is counterfeit money which, but for vanity, would have no circulation.

François de La Rochefoucauld

We refute praise from a desire to be praised twice.

François de La Rochefoucauld

Flattery

We sometimes think that we hate flattery, but we only hate the manner in which it is done.

François de La Rochefoucauld

He who praises you for what you lack wishes to take from you what you have.

Eugene Manuel

He soft-soaped her until she couldn't see for the suds.

Mary Roberts Rinehart

What really flatters a man is that you think him worth flattering.

George Bernard Shaw

Food

I would like to find a stew that will give me heartburn immediately instead of at three o'clock in the morning.

John Barrymore

Grub first, then ethics.

Bertolt Brecht

Few among those who go to restaurants realize
the man who first opened one must have been a
man of genius and a profound observer.

Anthelme Brillat-Savarin

Gastronomy rules all life: the newborn baby's
tears demand the nurse's breast, and the dying
man receives with some pleasure the last cooling
drink.

Anthelme Brillat-Savarin

Salt is the policeman of taste; it keeps the various
flavors of a dish in order and restrains the stronger
from tyrannizing over the weaker.

M. Chazal

Noncooks think it's silly to invest two hours'
work in two minutes' enjoyment; but if cooking is
evanescent, so is the ballet.

Julia Child

What my mother believed about cooking is that if
you worked hard and prospered, someone else
would do it for you.

Nora Ephron

Food

Food, love, career, and mothers, the four major guilt groups.

Cathy Guisewite

Let me smile with the wise and eat with the rich.

Samuel Johnson

The act of putting into your mouth what the earth has grown is perhaps your most direct inter-action with the earth.

Frances Moore Lappé

Everything you see I owe to spaghetti.

Sophia Loren

Fishes live in the sea as men do a-land; the big ones eat the little ones.

Pericles

There is no love sincerer than the love of food.

George Bernard Shaw

Bad men live that they may eat and drink, where-as good men eat and drink that they may live.

Socrates

Fool

Part of the secret of success in life is to eat what you like and let the food fight it out.

Mark Twain

To eat is human, to digest divine.

Mark Twain

See also DIET, HEALTH

Fool

A fellow who is always declaring he's no fool, usually has his suspicions.

Anonymous

A fool and his father's money can go places.

Anonymous

He who makes use of fools has to put up with them.

Cabillo de Aragon

A mother takes twenty years to make a man of her boy, and another woman makes a fool of him in twenty minutes.

Robert Frost

Fool

Let us be thankful for the fools. But for them, the rest of us could not succeed.

Robert Frost

In the days of Caesar, kings had fools and jesters. Now network presidents have anchormen.

Ted Koppel

Fortune, seeing that she could not make fools wise, has made them lucky.

Michel de Montaigne

For fools rush in where angels fear to tread.

Alexander Pope

Forgiving

Many promising reconciliations have broken down because while both parties came prepared to forgive, neither party came prepared to be forgiven.

Anonymous

I can pardon everyone's mistakes but my own.

Marcus Porcius Cato

His heart was as great as the world but there was no room in it to hold the memory of a wrong.

Robert Emerson

Forgive, but never forget.

John F. Kennedy

He who has not forgiven an enemy has not yet tasted one of the most sublime enjoyments of life.

Johann Lavater

See also BLAME, DEPRECATION, LOVE

Freedom

Only he is free who cultivates his own thoughts ... and strives without fear of man to do justice to them.

Berthold Auerbach

The wind is the only thing in civilization to enjoy freedom.

Elias Canetti

Freedom is not worth having if it does not connote freedom to err.

Mahatma Gandhi

Freedom

The basic test of freedom is perhaps less in what we are free to do than in what we are free not to do.

Eric Hoffer

We feel free when we escape, even if it be from the frying pan into the fire.

Eric Hoffer

Freedom is indivisible, and when one man is enslaved, all are not free.

John F. Kennedy

Freedom is only good as a means; it is no end in itself.

Herman Melville

A nation may lose its liberties in a day and not miss them for a century.

Baron de Montesquieu

Liberty is the right to tell people what they do not want to hear.

George Orwell

Those who expect to reap the blessings of freedom must, like men, undergo the fatigue of supporting it.

Thomas Paine

A hungry man is not a free man.

Adlai Stevenson

I don't think anyone is free. One creates one's own prison.

George Sutherland

To be free is to have achieved your life.

Tennessee Williams

Freedom has become as transparent as air, but it has also become as vital as air.

Boris Yeltsin

See also INDEPENDENCE, LIBERTY

Friendship

Everybody is not capable of being a friend, but everybody has it in his power to be an enemy.

Anonymous

Friendship

Choose your friends carefully. Your enemies will
choose you.

Yassir Arafat

Without friends, the world is but a wilderness.

Francis Bacon

Don't go to visit a friend in the hour of his
disgrace.

Rabbi Ben-Eleazer

How much easier to make pets of our friends'
weaknesses than to put up with strengths.

Elizabeth Bibesco

Of what help is anyone who can only be
approached with the right words?

Elizabeth Bibesco

It is easier to forgive an Enemy than to forgive a
Friend.

William Blake

Friendship may, and often does, grow into love,
but love never subsides into friendship.

Lord Byron

In prosperity our friends know us; in adversity we know our friends.

John Churton Collins

And if a friend does evil to you, say to him, "I forgive you for what you did to me, but how can I forgive you for what you did to yourself?"

Democritus

Go often to the house of a friend for weeds choke the unused path.

Ralph Waldo Emerson

It is not so much our friends' help that helps us as the confident knowledge that they will help us.

Epicurus

Since we are mortal, friendships are best kept to a moderate level, rather than sharing the very depths of our souls.

Euripides

There are three faithful friends—an old wife, an old dog, and ready money.

Benjamin Franklin

Friendship

True friendship comes when silence between two people is comfortable.

Dave Tyson Gentry

Life without a friend, death without a witness.

George Herbert

We have fewer friends than we imagine, but more than we know.

Hugo von Hofmannsthal

Friend: one who knows all about you and loves you just the same.

Elbert Hubbard

Friend is sometimes a word devoid of meaning; *enemy*, never.

Victor Hugo

He that has no one to love or confide in, has little to hope. He wants the radical principle of happiness.

Samuel Johnson

A true friend is the most precious of all possessions
and the one we take least thought about acquiring.

François de La Rochefoucauld

It is more shameful to distrust one's friends than
to be deceived by them.

François de La Rochefoucauld

When a man laughs at his troubles he loses a
good many friends. They never forgive the loss of
their prerogative.

H. L. Mencken

True friendship is never serene.

Marquise de Sévigné

Hearts that are delicate and kind and tongues that
are neither—these make the finest company in
the world.

Logan Pearsall Smith

Life is to be fortified by many friendships. To love,
and to be loved, is the greatest happiness of existence.

Sydney Smith

Friendship

So long as we love we serve; so long as we are loved by others, I would almost say that we are indispensable; and no man is useless while he has a friend.

Robert Louis Stevenson

Never speak ill of yourself; your friends will always say enough on that subject.

Charles Maurice de Talleyrand-Périgord

He makes no friend who never made a foe.

Alfred Lord Tennyson

Enemies publish themselves. They declare war. The friend never has to declare his love.

Henry David Thoreau

It takes your enemy and your friend, working together, to hurt you to the heart; the one to slander you and the other to get the news to you.

Mark Twain

The only safe and sure way to destroy an enemy is to make him your friend.

Mark Twain

If the first law of friendship is that it has to be cultivated, the second law is to be indulgent when the first law has been neglected.

Voltaire

If there were only two men in the world, how would they get on? They would help one another, harm one another, flatter one another, slander one another, fight one another, make it up; they could neither live together nor do without one another.

Voltaire

A real friend is one who walks in when the rest of the world walks out.

Walter Winchell

See also ENEMIES

Future

The best thing about the future is that it comes one day at a time.

Dean Acheson

Future

The future is like heaven—everyone exalts it but no one wants to go there now.

James Baldwin

The future is an opaque mirror. Anyone who tries to look into it sees nothing but the dim outlines of an old worried face.

Jim Bishop

I still lived in the future—a habit which is the death of happiness.

Quentin Crisp

The future is the past in preparation.

P. Dac

The strongest are those who renounce their own times and become a living part of those yet to come. The strongest and the rarest.

Milovan Djilas

Everyone's future is, in reality, an urn full of unknown treasures from which all may draw unguessed prizes.

Lord Dunsany

I never think of the future; it comes soon enough.

Albert Einstein

The danger of the past was that men became slaves. The danger of the future is that men may become robots.

Eric Fromm

This is my prediction for the future—whatever hasn't happened will happen and no one will be safe from it.

J. B. S. Haldane

I steer my bark with hope ahead and fear astern.

Thomas Jefferson

We should all be concerned about the future because we will have to spend the rest of our lives there.

Charles Kettering

It is bad enough to know the past; it would be intolerable to know the future.

W. Somerset Maugham

Future

We must take care that the forward movement does not degenerate into a headlong run. We must see to it that enthusiasm for the future does not give rise to contempt for the past.

Pope Paul VI

We can neither put back the clock nor slow down our forward speed, as we are already flying pilotless, on instrument controls, it is even too late to ask where we are going.

Igor Stravinsky

We often tend to be marching backward into the future.

Paul Valèry

I like men who have a future and women who have a past.

Oscar Wilde

Gambling

The gambling known as business looks with severe disfavor on the business known as gambling.

Ambrose Bierce

Gambling promises for the poor what property performs for the rich—something for nothing.

George Bernard Shaw

The roulette table pays nobody except him that keeps it. Nevertheless, a passion for gambling is common, though a passion for keeping roulette tables is unknown.

George Bernard Shaw

If you bet a horse, that's gambling. If you bet you can make three spades, that's entertainment. If you bet cotton will go up three points, that's business. See the difference?

William Sherrod

There are two times in a man's life when he should not speculate—when he can't afford it, and when he can.

Mark Twain

Genius

Genius may have its limitations but stupidity is not this handicapped.

Elbert Hubbard

Genius

The principal mark of genius is not perfection but originality, the opening of new frontiers.

Arthur Koestler

Sometimes men come by the name of genius in the same way that certain insects come by the name of centipede—not because they have a hundred feet, but because most people can't count above fourteen.

Georg Christoph Lichtenberg

When a true genius appears in the world, you know him by this sign, that the dunces are all in confederacy against him.

Jonathan Swift

Caricature is the tribute that mediocrity pays to genius.

Oscar Wilde

I have nothing to declare but my genius.

Oscar Wilde

See also TALENT

Giving

To enjoy a good reputation, give publicly, and
steal privately.

S. Billinger

One can know nothing of giving aught that is
worthy to give unless one also knows how to take.

Havelock Ellis

Take egotism out and you would castrate the
benefactors.

Ralph Waldo Emerson

The only gift is a portion of thyself.

Ralph Waldo Emerson

We often borrow from our tomorrows to pay our
debts to our yesterdays.

Khalil Gibran

You are indeed charitable when you give, and,
while giving, turn your face away so that you may
not see the shyness of the receiver.

Khalil Gibran

Giving

It is better to deserve without receiving than to receive without deserving.

Robert Ingersoll

Philanthropy is commendable, but it must not cause the philanthropist to overlook the circumstances of economic injustice which make philanthropy necessary.

Martin Luther King, Jr.

If the enemy be hungry, give him bread to eat; and if he be thirsty, give him water to drink.

Proverbs 25:21

We like the gift when we the giver prize.

John Sheffield

You must be fit to give before you can be fit to receive.

James Stephens

God

This only denied to God: the power to undo the past.

Agathon

All things bright and beautiful,
All creatures great and small,
All things wise and wonderful,
The Lord God made them all.

Cecil Frances Alexander

To my mind the most poignant mystical exhortation
ever written is "Be still and know that I am God."

Arnold Bennett

I respect the idea of God too much to hold it
responsible for a world as absurd as this one.

Georges Bumahel

God was satisfied with his own work, and that is
fatal.

Samuel Butler

If God were suddenly condemned to live the life
which he has inflicted on men, He would kill
Himself.

Alexandre Dumas, fils

If I were a nightingale, I would sing like a
nightingale; if a swan like a swan. But, since I am
a rational creature, my role is to praise God.

Epictetus

God

It is hard to believe in God, but it is far harder to disbelieve in him.

Harry Emerson Fosdick

The impotence of God is infinite.

Anatole France

Many a long dispute among divines may be thus abridged: it is so. It is not so. It is so. It is not so.

Benjamin Franklin

Man is a dog's ideal of what God should be.

Helen Jackson

Man considers the actions, but God weighs the intentions.

Thomas à Kempis

Every night, I still ask the Lord, "Why?" and I haven't heard a decent answer yet.

Jack Kerouac

It is very dangerous to go into eternity with possibilities which one has oneself prevented from becoming realities. A possibility is a hint from God.

Søren Kierkegaard

God seems to have left the receiver off the hook
and time is running out.

Arthur Koestler

God dwells wherever man lets him in.

Mendel of Kotzk

All gods were immortal.

Stanislaw Lec

God is a concept by which we measure our pain.

John Lennon

We have no choice but to be guilty. God is
unthinkable if we are innocent.

Archibald MacLeish

If on Judgment Day, I was confronted with God
and I found God took himself seriously, I would
like to go to the other place.

Malcom Muggeridge

Of course he [God] will forgive me; that's his
business.

Friedrich Wilhelm Nietzsche

God

The sufferer alone is permitted to praise God in his works. But all men suffer.

Franz Rosenzweig

Live among men as if God beheld you; speak to God as if men were listening.

Seneca

An atheist is a person who has no invisible means of support.

Fulton J. Sheen

God is a writer, and we are both heroes and the readers.

Isaac Bashevis Singer

God wants the heart.

The Talmud

God has not called me to be successful; he has called me to be faithful.

Mother Theresa

He who knows about depth, knows about God.

Paul Tillich

God made everything out of nothing. But the nothingness shows through.

Paul Valéry

God's contempt for human minds is evidenced by miracles. He judges them unworthy of being drawn to Him by other means than those of stupefaction and the crudest modes of sensibility.

Paul Valéry

God gives himself to men as powerful or perfect. It is for them to choose.

Simone Weil

The Ethiopians say that their gods are snub-nosed and black, the Thracians that theirs have light blue eyes and red hair.

Xenophanes

See also AFTERLIFE, BELIEFS, BIBLE, ETERNITY, FAITH, HELL, MORALITY, RELIGION

Goodwill

Moral of the Work. In war: resolution. In defeat: defiance. In victory: magnanimity. In peace: good-will.

Winston Churchill

The most precious thing anyone, man or business, anybody or anything, can have is the goodwill of others.

Anne Parish

You are not only good yourself, but the cause of goodness in others.

Socrates

Be not simply good. Be good for something.

Henry David Thoreau

To be good is noble, but to show others how to be good is nobler and no trouble.

Mark Twain

See also *EVIL, HATE, KINDNESS*

Government

No government can be long secure without formidable opposition.

Benjamin Disraeli

The best government is not that which renders
men the happiest but that which renders the
greatest number happy.

Charles-Pinot Duclos

You cannot extend the mastery of government
over the daily working life of people without at
the same time making it the master of people's
souls and thoughts.

Herbert Hoover

I see the President and the First Lady are not
here—probably someplace testifying.

Don Imus

He that would govern others, first should be
The master of himself.

Philip Massinger

Government

I can govern the United States or I can govern my daughter, Alice, but I can't do both.

Theodore Roosevelt

No man undertakes a trade he has not learned, even the meanest. Yet everyone thinks himself sufficiently qualified for the hardest of all trades, that of government.

Socrates

The hardest thing about any political campaign is how to win without proving that you are unworthy in the winning.

Adlai Stevenson

Every man who takes office in Washington either grows or swells.

Woodrow Wilson

See also COMMITTEES, DEMOCRACY, DIPLOMATS, POLITICS

Gratitude

Next to ingratitude, the most painful thing is . . . gratitude.

Henry Ward Beecher

Gratitude is when memory is stored in the heart and not in the mind.

Lionel Hampton

Gratitude is a useless word. You will find it in a dictionary but not in life.

François de La Rochefoucauld

Gratitude is the most exquisite form of courtesy.

Jacques Maritain

Greatness

A one-eyed man is king in the land of the blind.

Anonymous

Greatness lies not in being strong, but in the right use of strength.

Henry Ward Beecher

No great man lives in vain. The history of the world is but the biography of great men.

Thomas Carlyle

No really great man ever thought himself so.

William Hazlitt

Greatness

The greatest truths are the simplest, and so are the greatest men.

Joseph Howe

Great minds have purposes; others have wishes.

Washington Irving

He was dull in a new way, and that made many think him great.

Samuel Johnson

An occasional weakness in a great man is a comfort to the rest of us.

Herbert Prochnow

Be not afraid of greatness: some are born great; some achieve greatness, and some have greatness thrust upon them.

William Shakespeare: Twelfth Night

One of the signs of Napoleon's greatness is the fact that he once had a publisher shot.

Siegfried Unseld

See also EGO

Grief

It is dangerous to abandon oneself to the luxury of grief: it deprives one of courage, and even of the wish for recovery.

Henri-Frédéric Amiel

It is foolish to tear one's hair in grief, as though sorrow would be made less with baldness.

Cicero

One can bear grief, but it takes two to be glad.

Elbert Hubbard

No one ever told me that grief felt so like fear.

C. S. Lewis

Excess of grief for the deceased is madness, for it is an injury to the living, and the dead know it not.

Xenophanes

See also FEELINGS, SORROW, SUFFERING

Habit

Chaos often breeds life, when order breeds habit.

Henry Adams

When one begins to live by habit and by quotation, one has begun to stop living.

James Baldwin

The fixity of habit is generally in direct proportion to its absurdity.

Marcel Proust

I believe that the mind can be permanently profaned by the habit of attending to trivial things so that all our thoughts shall be tinged with triviality.

Henry David Thoreau

Happiness

A large income is the best recipe for happiness I ever heard of.

Jane Austen

Happiness: an agreeable sensation arising from contemplating the misery of others.

Ambrose Bierce

The secret of happiness is to admire without desiring. And that is not happiness.

F. H. Bradley

There is no happiness that is not idleness and only what is useless is pleasurable.

Anton Chekhov

The poor man is happy; he expects no change for the worse.

Demetrius

The sense of existence is the greatest happiness.

Benjamin Disraeli

Happiness is a perfume you cannot pour on others without getting a few drops on yourself.

Ralph Waldo Emerson

Happiness

Whoever is happy will make others happy too. He who has courage and faith will never perish in misery.

Anne Frank

A happy life is one spent in learning, earning and yearning.

Lillian Gish

There is no such thing as the pursuit of happiness, but there is the discovery of joy.

J. Grentell

There is an hour wherein a man might be happy all his life, could he find it.

George Herbert

Happiness is how, not a what: a talent, not an object.

Hermann Hesse

To be able to throw oneself away for the sake of a moment, to be able to sacrifice years for a woman's smile—that is happiness.

Hermann Hesse

It's pretty hard to tell what does bring happiness.
Poverty and wealth have both failed.

Elbert Hubbard

The happiest people seem to be those who have
no particular reason for being happy except that
they are so.

William Inge

Happiness grows at our own firesides and is not
to be picked in strangers' gardens.

D. Jerrard

We dream those happy who from the experience
of life have learned to bear its ills without being
overcome by them.

Juvenal

One kind of happiness is to know exactly at what
point to be miserable.

François de La Rochefoucauld

Most folks are about as happy as they make up
their minds to be.

Abraham Lincoln

Happiness

It's good to have money and the things that money can buy but it's good to check up once in a while to make sure you haven't lost the things that money can't buy.

George Claude Lorimer

Extremely happy and extremely unhappy men are alike prone to grow hard-hearted.

Baron de Montesquieu

If we only wanted to be happy, it would be easy; but we want to be happier than other people, and that is almost always difficult, since we think them happier than they are.

Baron de Montesquieu

The only way to avoid being miserable is not to have enough leisure to wonder whether you are happy or not.

George Bernard Shaw

No man is happy; he is at best fortunate.

Solon

Happiness is a perpetual possession of being well-deceived.

Jonathan Swift

The purpose of life is the expansion of happiness.

Maharishi Mahesh Yogi

See also FEELINGS, JOY, PLEASURE

Hardship

Adversity is the first path to truth.

Anonymous

The times are not so bad as they seem; they couldn't be.

Anonymous

Half a calamity is better than a whole one.

Lawrence of Arabia

Ad astra per aspera. [To the stars through hard-ships.]

Latin proverb

Hardship

Adversity reminds men of religion.

Livy

No pain, no palm; no thorns, no throne; no gall,
no glory; no cross, no crown.

William Penn

See also TROUBLES

Hate

Let them hate, so long as they fear.

Lucius Accius

Hatred, which could destroy so much, never failed
to destroy the man who hated and this was an
immutable law.

James Baldwin

No hatred is by far the longest pleasure;
Men love in haste, but they detest at leisure.

Lord Byron

He that fears you present will hate you absent.

Thomas Fuller

Impotent hatred is the most horrid of all emotions; one should hate nobody whom one cannot destroy.

Johann Wolfgang von Goethe

If a man say, I love God, and hateth his brother, he is a liar. He that loveth not his brother whom he hath seen, how can he love God whom he hath not seen?

1 John 4:20

Hate is always a clash between our spirit and someone else's body.

Cesare Pavese

Like the greatest virtue and the worst dogs, the fiercest hatred is silent.

Jean Paul Richter

See also FEELINGS, GOODWILL, LOVE, REVENGE

Health

Health is infinite and expansive in mode, and reaches out to be filled with the fullness of the world; whereas the disease is finite and reductive

in mode, and endeavors to reduce the world
to itself.

Anonymous

There's lots of people who spend so much time
watching their health, they haven't time to
enjoy it.

Josh Billings

Thousands upon thousands of persons have studied disease. Almost no one has studied health.

Adelle Davis

Wisdom is to the soul what health is to the body.

De Saint-Real

Your body is the baggage you must carry through
life. The more excess baggage the shorter the trip.

A. Glasgow

The body never lies.

Martha Graham

To safeguard one's health at the cost of too strict a
diet is a tiresome illness indeed.

François de La Rochefoucauld

If you want to live, you must walk. If you want to live long, you must run.

J. Navik

Illness is a great leveler. At its touch, the artificial distinctions of society vanish away. People in a hospital are just people.

M. Thorek

For fast-acting relief, try slowing down.

Lily Tomlin

A man who is "of sound mind" is one who keeps the inner madman under lock and key.

Paul Valéry

See also BODY, DIET, DISEASE, DOCTORS, FOOD, INSANITY

Heart

The mother's heart is the child's schoolroom.

Henry Ward Beecher

The world either breaks or hardens the heart.

Nicolas Chamfort

Heart

If you look into your own heart, and you find nothing wrong there, what is there to worry about? What is there to fear?

Confucius

The nearest to my heart are a king without a kingdom and a poor man who does not know how to beg.

Khalil Gibran

A slimy, throbbing mass of muscle entwined in its own veins and arteries, a tender, fearsome instrument of love and power—the heart!

George Leonard

Hell

Hell, madame, is to love no longer.

Georges Bernanos

I believe in heaven and hell, on earth.

Abraham Feinberg

Maybe this world is another planet's Hell.

Aldous Huxley

The road to hell is paved with good intentions.

Karl Marx

Men have fiendishly conceived a heaven, only to find it insipid, and a hell only to find it ridiculous.

George Santayana

I never did give anyone hell. I just told the truth, and they thought it was hell.

Harry Truman

See also *AFTERLIFE, BIBLE, CHRISTIANITY, GOD*

Heroism

Show me a hero and I will write you a tragedy.

F. Scott Fitzgerald

To bear other people's afflictions, everyone has courage and enough to spare.

Benjamin Franklin

As you get older, it is harder to have heroes, but it is sort of necessary.

Ernest Hemingway

Heroism

In war, the heroes always outnumber the soldiers ten to one.

H. L. Mencken

I still think the movie heroes are in the audience.

Wilson Mizner

Kill reverence and you have killed the hero in a man.

Edward Rand

Being a hero is about the shortest lived profession on earth.

Will Rogers

We can't all be heroes because someone has to sit on the curb and clap as they go by.

Will Rogers

See also WAR

History

All history is the propaganda of the victorious.

Anonymous

Do not seek to follow in the footsteps of the men of old; seek what they sought.

Matsuo Basho

History: an account mostly false of events unimportant which are brought about by rulers mostly knaves and soldiers mostly fools.

Ambrose Bierce

The main thing is to make history, not to write it.

Otto von Bismarck

God cannot alter the past, but historians can.

Samuel Butler

History will absolve me.

Fidel Castro

History is the transformation of tumultuous conquerors into silent footnotes.

Paul Eldridge

In analyzing history, do not be too profound, for often the causes are quite superficial.

Ralph Waldo Emerson

History

Our ignorance of history makes us libel our own times. People have always been like this.

Gustave Flaubert

It takes time to ruin a world, but time is all it takes.

Bernard Fontenelle

Ask counsel of the Ancients, what is best; but of the Moderns, what is fittest.

Thomas Fuller

The greatest of men are always linked to their age by some weakness or other.

Johann Wolfgang von Goethe

Just as philosophy is the study of other people's misconceptions, so history is the study of other people's mistakes.

Phillip Guedalla

By despising all that has preceded us, we teach others to despise ourselves.

William Hazlitt

The history of humankind is a repository of scuttled objective truths and a museum of irrefutable facts, refuted not by empirical discoveries, but by man's mysterious decisions to experience differently from time to time.

Friedrich Heller

Very few things happen at the right time, and the rest do not happen at all. The conscientious historian will correct these defects.

Herodotus

Men are more like the times they live in than they are like their fathers.

Ali Ibn-Abi-Talib

The people who live in a Golden Age usually go around complaining how yellow everything looks.

Randall Jarrell

We have the power to make this the best generation of mankind in the history of the world, or the last.

John F. Kennedy

History

History knows no resting places and no plateaus.

Henry Kissinger

Perhaps in time the so-called dark ages will be thought of as including our own.

Georg Christoph Lichtenberg

Throughout history the world has been laid waste to ensure the triumph of conceptions that are now as dead as the men that died for them.

Henry de Montherlant

Men after death are understood worse than men of the moment, but heard better.

Friedrich Wilhelm Nietzsche

Each generation imagines itself to be more intelligent than the one that went before it and wiser than the one that comes after it.

George Orwell

The only thing that does not change is that at any and every time it appears that there have been "great changes."

Marcel Proust

Those who cannot remember the past are condemned to repeat it.

George Santayana

The man who sees two or three generations is like someone who sits in a conjurer's booth at a fair and sees the tricks two or three times. They are meant to be seen only once.

Arthur Schopenhauer

The novelties of one generation are only the resuscitated fashions of one generation before last.

George Bernard Shaw

We are the children of our age, but children who can never know their mother.

Lillian Smith

The greatest inventions were produced in the times of ignorance, as the use of the compass, gunpowder, and printing.

Jonathan Swift

The certainties of one age are the problems of the next.

Richard H. Tawney

History

To give an accurate description of what never happened is the proper occupation of the historian.

Oscar Wilde

What is amusing now had to be taken in desperate earnest once.

Virginia Woolf

Hollywood

Nobody sets out to make a bad picture.

Anonymous

It's slave labor and what do you get for it? A lousy fortune!

Samuel Nathaniel Behrman

You can have the best producer and the best director but it won't make any difference if you don't have the story.

Marie Dressler

A verbal contract isn't worth the paper it's written on.

Samuel Goldwyn

The propaganda arm of the American Dream machine, Hollywood.

Molly Haskell

Millions are to be grabbed out here and your only competition is idiots.

Herbert Mankiewicz

No matter how hot it gets in the daytime in Hollywood it's always dull at night.

Sam Marx

You're only as good as your last picture.

Sam Marx

There's nothing wrong with this business that a good picture won't cure.

Nicholas M. Schenk

Audiences will reach for quality but never stoop.

Irving Thalberg

See also *ACTING, DRAMA, FILMS, TALENT, TELEVISION*

Hope

Hope is a waking dream.

Aristotle

Hope is a good breakfast, but it is a bad supper.

Francis Bacon

We often call a certainty a hope, to bring it luck.

Elizabeth Bibesco

If you do not hope, you will not find what is beyond your hopes.

St. Clement

The mind that renounces once and forever a futile hope has its compensation in ever-growing calm.

George Gissing

Hope is generally a wrong guide, though it is very good company by the way.

Lord Halifax

Men should do with their hopes as they do with tame fowl: cut their wings that they may not fly over the wall.

Lord Halifax

Walk on, walk on, with hope in your heart;
and you'll never walk alone; you'll never walk
alone.

Oscar Hammerstein II

The sudden disappointment of a hope leaves a
scar which the ultimate fulfillment of that hope
never entirely removes.

Thomas Hardy

Hope is itself a species of happiness and perhaps
the chief happiness which this world affords.

Samuel Johnson

The natural flights of the human mind are not
from pleasure to pleasure, but from hope to hope.

Samuel Johnson

Our hopes, often though they deceive us, lead us
pleasantly along the path of life.

François de La Rochefoucauld

"Blessed is the man who expects nothing, for he
shall never be disappointed" was the ninth beatitude.

Alexander Pope

Hope

A cathedral, a wave of a storm, a dancer's leap,
never turn out to be as high as we had hoped.

Marcel Proust

In the factory we make cosmetics; in the store we
sell hope.

Charles Revson

Honor begets honor; trust begets trust; faith
begets faith, and hope is the mainspring of life.

Henry L. Stimson

The most absurd and the most rash hopes have
sometimes been the cause of extraordinary
success.

Marquis de Vauvenargues

Vows begin when hope dies.

Leonardo da Vinci

We are all in the gutter, but some of us are looking at the stars.

Oscar Wilde

See also DREAMS, FEELINGS, OPTIMISM

Humor

Fun I love, but too much fun is of all things the most loathsome. Mirth is better than fun, and happiness is better than humor.

William Blake

We must laugh at a man to avoid crying for him.

Napoleon Bonaparte

If you want to make people weep, you must weep yourself. If you want to make people laugh, your face must remain serious.

Casanova

Sentimental irony is a dog that bays at a moon while he pisses on a grave.

Craus

Humor is by far the most significant activity of the human brain.

Edward De Bono

A comedian does funny things; a good comedian does things funny.

Buster Keaton

Humor

A joke is a kind of coitus interruptus between reason and emotion.

Arthur Koestler

Everything is funny as long as it is happening to somebody else.

Will Rogers

Jesters do oft prove prophets.

William Shakespeare: King Lear

My way of joking is telling the truth; that is the funniest joke in the world.

George Bernard Shaw

It's hard to be funny if you have to be clean.

Mae West

See also LAUGHTER

Husbands

Grandchildren don't make a man feel old; it's the knowledge that he's married to a grandmother.

G. Norman Collie

The calmest husbands make the stormiest wives.

Thomas Dekker

The better the workman, the worse husband.

Thomas Draxe

Wives, submit yourselves unto your own husbands, as unto the Lord. For the husband is the head of the wife, even as Christ is the head of the church . . .

Ephesians 5:22–23

God, give me a rich husband though he be an ass.

Thomas Fuller

He knows little who will tell his wife all he knows.

Thomas Fuller

Husbands are like fires. They go out if unattended.

Zsa Zsa Gabor

Husband and wife come to look alike at last.

Oliver Wendell Holmes

Husbands

A man should be taller, older, heavier, uglier, and hoarser than his wife.

Edgar Watson Howe

There is only one thing to do for a man who is married to a woman who enjoys spending money, and that is to enjoy earning it.

Edgar Watson Howe

Do married men make the best husbands?

James Gibbons Huneker

Upon a man and his wife a husband's infidelity is nothing.

Samuel Johnson

There are few women so perfect that their husbands do not regret having married them at least once a day.

Jean de La Bruyère

Serve your husband as your master, and beware of him as a traitor.

Michel de Montaigne

A man must ask his wife's leave to thrive.

John Ray

A husband is what is left of a man after the nerve is extracted.

Helen Rowland

A light wife doth make a heavy husband.

William Shakespeare: Merchant of Venice

Thy husband is thy lord, thy life, thy keeper.

William Shakespeare: The Taming of the Shrew

A husband and wife ought to continue so long united as they love each other.

Percy Bysshe Shelley

As the husband is, the wife is.

Alfred Lord Tennyson

One can always recognize women who trust their husbands. They look so thoroughly unhappy.

Oscar Wilde

See also BACHELORS, MAN, MARRIAGE, WIVES

Hypocrisy

I have seen hypocrisy that was so artful that it was good judgment to be deceived by it.

Josh Billings

Man is the only animal that can remain on friendly terms with the victims he intends to eat.

Samuel Butler

Be on your guard against those who confess as their weaknesses all the cardinal virtues.

Lord Chesterfield

Is it not possible to eat me without insisting that I sing the praises of my devourer?

Feodor Dostoyevsky

Clean your finger before you point at my spots.

Benjamin Franklin

Many kiss the hand they wish cut off.

George Herbert

No man is a hypocrite in his pleasures.

Samuel Johnson

Hypocrisy is the homage that vice pays to virtue.

François de La Rochefoucauld

A hypocrite is a person who ... but who isn't?

Don Marquis

I despise the pleasure of pleasing people whom I despise.

Michel de Montaigne

Few men speak humbly of humility, chastely of chastity, skeptically of skepticism.

Blaise Pascal

With people of limited ability, modesty is merely honesty; but with those who possess great talent, it is hypocrisy.

Arthur Schopenhauer

You can't eat your friends and have them too.

Budd Schulberg

The value of an idea has nothing to do with the success of the man who expresses it.

Oscar Wilde

See also DECEPTION, LYING, SINCERITY

Ideals

Idealism increases in direct proportion to one's distance from the problem.

John Galsworthy

When a man forgets his ideals, he may hope for happiness, but not till then.

John Oliver Hobbes

The idealist is incorrigible. If he is turned out of his heaven, he makes an ideal of his hell.

Friedrich Wilhelm Nietzsche

In our ideals we unwittingly reveal our vices.

Jean Rostand

Ideals are thoughts. So long as they exist merely as thoughts, the power in them remains ineffective.

Albert Schweitzer

When they come downstairs from their Ivory Tower, idealists are apt to walk straight into the gutter.

Logan Pearsall Smith

See also BELIEFS

Ideas

Nothing is more dangerous than an idea when it's the only one we have.

Alain

The wise only possess ideas; the greater part of mankind is possessed by them.

Anonymous

There is no adequate defense, except stupidity, against the impact of a new idea.

Percy Williams Bridgeman

It is the idea, the feeling and the love God means mankind should strive for and show forth.

Robert Browning

Ideas must work through the brains and arms of men, or they are no better than dreams.

Ralph Waldo Emerson

Having ideas is like having chessmen moving forward; they may be beaten, but they may start a winning game.

Johann Wolfgang von Goethe

Ideas

That fellow seems to me to possess but one idea, and that is a wrong one.

Samuel Johnson

The idea wants changelessness and eternity. Whoever lives under the supremacy of the idea strives for permanence; hence, everything that pushes toward change must be against it.

Carl Jung

The power of vested interests is vastly exaggerated compared with the gradual encroachment of ideas.

John Maynard Keynes

Folly is our constant companion throughout life; if someone appears wise, it is only because his follies are suited to his age and station.

François de La Rochefoucauld

When he was expected to use his mind, he felt like a right-handed person who has to do something with his left.

Georg Christoph Lichtenberg

Ideas

It is not in the power of the most exalted wit or enlarged understanding, by any quickness of variety of thought, to invent or frame one new simple idea.

John Locke

An idea that is not dangerous is unworthy of being called an idea at all.

Don Marquis

The ruling ideas of each age have ever been the ideas of its ruling class.

Karl Marx

To accept an unorthodoxy is always to inherit unresolved contradictions.

George Orwell

A powerful idea communicates some of its power to the man who contradicts it.

Marcel Proust

A man is infinitely more complicated than his thoughts.

Paul Valéry

Ideas

The history of thought may be summed up in these words: it is absurd by what it seeks, great by what it finds.

Paul Valéry

See also REASON, THOUGHT

Idleness

An idler is a watch that wants both hands, as useless if it goes as if it stands.

William Cowper

A loafer always has the correct time.

Kin (Frank McKinney) Hubbard

It is impossible to enjoy idling thoroughly unless one has plenty of work to do.

Jerome K. Jerome

Every man is or hopes to be, an idler.

Samuel Johnson

To be idle and to be poor have always been reproaches and therefore every man endeavors with his utmost care to hide his poverty from others and his idleness from himself.

Samuel Johnson

Rushing to and fro, busily employed in idleness.

Phaedrus

There is no pleasure in having nothing to do; the fun is in having lots to do and not doing it.

J. Raper

It is difficult to keep quiet if you have nothing to do.

Arthur Schopenhauer

See also LAZINESS, LEISURE

Ignorance

To be ignorant of one's ignorance is the malady of the ignorant.

Bronson Alcott

It is better to know nothing than to know what ain't so.

Josh Billings

Ignorance

The Skeptics that affirmed they knew nothing,
even in that opinion confused themselves and
thought they knew more than all the world
beside.

Sir Thomas Browne

That there should one man die ignorant who had
capacity for knowledge, this I call a tragedy.

Thomas Carlyle

Ignorance gives one a large range of probabilities.

George Eliot

There are many things of which a wise man
might wish to be ignorant.

Ralph Waldo Emerson

Ignorance is the necessary condition of life itself.
If we knew everything, we could not endure existence for a single hour.

Anatole France

Ignorance is ignorance; no right to believe anything can be derived from it.

Sigmund Freud

He that knows little often repeats it.

Thomas Fuller

Nothing is more terrible than ignorance in action.

Johann Wolfgang von Goethe

Where ignorance is bliss, 'tis folly to be wise.

Thomas Gray

A man's ignorance is as much his private property and as precious in his own eyes as his family Bible.

Oliver Wendell Holmes

Your ignorance cramps my conversation.

Bob Hope

Even supposing knowledge to be easily attainable, more people would be content to be ignorant than would take even a little trouble to acquire it.

Samuel Johnson

Ignorance

Ignorance cannot always be inferred from inaccuracy; knowledge is not always present.

Samuel Johnson

Ignorance, madame, pure ignorance.

Samuel Johnson

Art hath an enemy called Ignorance.

Ben Jonson

Nothing in all the world is more dangerous than sincere ignorance and conscientious stupidity.

Martin Luther King, Jr.

Ignorance is the mother of all evils.

Michel de Montaigne

There is an ABC ignorance which precedes knowledge and doctoral ignorance which comes after it.

Michel de Montaigne

Ignorance is of a peculiar nature; once dispelled, it is impossible to reestablish it.

Thomas Paine

If you are ignorant, you certainly can get into some interesting arguments.

Herbert Prochnow

Ignorance is degrading only when found in company with riches.

Arthur Schopenhauer

It may be that the ignorant man, alone, has any chance to mate his life with life.

Wallace Stevens

Blind and naked Ignorance
Delivers brawling judgments,
unashamed.

Alfred Lord Tennyson

I would rather have my ignorance than another man's knowledge, because I have so much of it.

Mark Twain

That man must be tremendously ignorant: he answers every question that is put to him.

Voltaire

Ignorance

I do not approve of anything which tampers with
natural ignorance.

Oscar Wilde

See also EDUCATION, KNOWLEDGE

Imagination

Where there is no imagination there is no horror.

Sir Arthur Conan Doyle

There is a space between man's imagination and
man's attainment that may only be traversed by
his longing.

Khalil Gibran

Were it not for imagination, sir, a man would be
as happy in the arms of a chambermaid as a
duchess.

Samuel Johnson

Without this playing with fantasy no creative
work has ever yet come to birth. The debt we
owe to the play of imagination is incalculable.

Carl Jung

Imitation

Imitation is the sincerest form of flattery.

Charles Caleb Colton

When people are free to do as they please, they usually imitate each other.

Eric Hoffer

No man ever yet became great by imitation.

Samuel Johnson

Independence

I once worked as a salesman and was very independent. I took orders from no one.

Jacques Barzun

If money is your hope for independence, you will never have it.

Henry Ford

Neither the clamor of the mob nor the voice of power will ever turn me by the breadth of a hair from the course I made out for myself guided by

Independence

such knowledge as I can obtain and controlled and directed by a solemn conviction of right and duty.

Robert La Follette

When I was a boy, I used to do what my father wanted. Now I have to do what my boy wants. My problem is: when am I going to do what I want?

Sam Levinson

See also FREEDOM, LIBERTY

Individualism

No one ever heard of state freedom, much less did anyone ever hear of state morals. Freedom and morals are the exclusive possession of individuals.

Anonymous

Resolve to be thyself and know that he who finds himself loves his misery.

Matthew Arnold

We all come down to dinner, but each has a room to himself.

Walter Bagehot

To be happy, we must not be too concerned with others.

Albert Camus

We forfeit three-fourths of ourselves in order to be like other people.

Arthur Schopenhauer

There will never be a really free and enlightened state until the state comes to recognize the individual as a higher and independent power from which all its own power and authority are derived and treats him accordingly.

Henry David Thoreau

See also CHARACTER, CONFORMITY, ORIGINALITY

Inflation

The first panacea for a mismanaged nation is inflation of the currency. The second is war. Both bring a temporary prosperity; both bring a permanent ruin.

Ernest Hemingway

Inflation

We have two chickens in every pot, two cars in every garage, and now we have two headaches for every aspirin.

Fiorello H. La Guardia

Inflation is as violent as a mugger, as frightening as an armed robber and as deadly as a hit man.

Ronald Reagan

The nation is prosperous on the whole, but how much prosperity is there in a hole?

Will Rogers

Insanity

Only the insane take themselves seriously.

Max Beerbohm

I sometimes wonder whether our planet is the asylum of our universe for disordered minds.

Johann Wolfgang von Goethe

Insanity is often the logic of an accurate mind overtaxed.

Oliver Wendell Holmes

Insanity is hereditary. You can get it from your kids.

Sam Levinson

See also HEALTH, REASON

Intelligence

An intelligent person often talks with his eyes; a shallow man often swallows with his ears.

Anonymous

It is better not to reflect at all than not to reflect enough.

Tristan Bernard

Wisdom cannot create materials; they are the gifts of nature or chance; her pride is in the use.

Edmund Burke

Wit without employment is a disease.

Robert Burton

A man is not necessarily intelligent because he has plenty of ideas any more than he is a good general because he has plenty of soldiers.

Nicolas Chamfort

Intelligence

Merely having an open mind is nothing. The object of opening the mind, as of opening the mouth, is to shut it again on something solid.

G. K. Chesterton

It is not enough to have a good mind. The main thing is to use it well.

René Descartes

I suppose you could never prove to the mind of the ingenuous mollusk that such a creature as a whale was possible.

Ralph Waldo Emerson

Many would be wise if they did not think themselves wise.

Baltasar Gracián

You should never be clever but when you cannot help it.

Richard Fulke Greville

There is nobody so irritating as somebody with less intelligence and more sense than we have.

David E. Herold

You cannot gauge the intelligence of an American by talking with him.

Eric Hoffer

A moment's insight is sometimes worth a life's experience.

Oliver Wendell Holmes

Such is the delight of mental superiority that none on whom nature or study have conferred it would purchase the gifts of fortune by its loss.

Samuel Johnson

The voice of intelligence . . . is drowned out by the roar of fear . . . Most of all it is silenced by ignorance.

Karl Menninger

A really intelligent man feels what other men only know.

Baron de Montesquieu

The more intelligent one is, the more men of originality one finds. Ordinary people find no dif-ference between men.

Blaise Pascal

Intelligence

At a certain age, some people's minds close up.
They live on their intellectual fat.

William Lyon Phelps

A man should never be ashamed to own that he
has been in the wrong, which is but saying, in
other words, that he is wiser today than he was
yesterday.

Alexander Pope

The more unintelligent a man is, the less mysterious existence seems to him.

Arthur Schopenhauer

There is something in us wiser than our head.

Arthur Schopenhauer

A man's intelligence does not increase as he
acquires power. What does increase is the diffi-
culty in telling him so.

D. Southerland

All this worldly wisdom was once the unamiable
heresy of some wise man.

Henry David Thoreau

A great many people think that polysyllables are a sign of intelligence.

Barbara Walters

See also MIND, THOUGHT

Israel

In Israel, in order to be a realist, you must believe in miracles.

David Ben-Gurion

Israel cannot defend itself if half its population is the enemy.

Yehoshafat Harkabi

The only thing chicken about Israel is their soup.

Bob Hope

If Moses had been a committee, the Israelites would still be in Egypt.

Johnson Donald Hughes

When Arthur Balfour launched his scheme for peopling Palestine with Jewish immigrants I am

credibly informed that he did not know there
were Arabs in the country.

William Inge

We Jews have a secret weapon in our struggle
with the Arabs; we have no place to go.

Golda Meir

When peace comes we will perhaps, in time, be
able to forgive the Arabs for killing our sons, but
it will be harder for us to forgive them for having
forced us to kill their sons.

Golda Meir

Jealousy

Envy is a pain of mind that successful men cause
their neighbors.

Anonymous

Jealousy is nothing more than the fear of aban-
donment.

Anonymous

Yet he was jealous, though he did not show it,
For jealousy dislikes the world to know it.

Lord Byron

Jealousy, the jaundice of the soul.

John Dryden

Lots of people know a good thing the minute the
other fellow sees it first.

Job Hedges

Jealousy is all the fun you think they had.

Erica Jong

In jealousy there is more self-love than love.

François de La Rochefoucauld

Jealousy is always born with love, but does not
always die with it.

François de La Rochefoucauld

To jealousy, nothing is more frightful than
laughter.

Françoise Sagan

Jealousy

O! beware, my lord, of jealousy;
It is the green-eyed monster which doth mock
The meat it feeds on . . .

William Shakespeare: Othello

Jealousy is cruel as the grave.

Song of Solomon 8:6

Moral indignation is jealousy with a halo.

H. G. Wells

Plain women are always jealous of their husbands,
beautiful women never are. They are always so
occupied with being jealous of other women's
husbands.

Oscar Wilde

See also ENVY, FEELINGS

Jobs

Housekeeping ain't no joke.

Anonymous

The heart to conceive, the understanding to
direct, and the hand to execute.

Anonymous

The test of a vocation is the love of the drudgery
it involves.

Anonymous

So much of what we call management consists in
making it difficult for people to work.

Peter Drucker

Our chief want in life is somebody who shall
make us do what we can.

Ralph Waldo Emerson

The difference between a job and a career is the
difference between forty and sixty hours a week.

Robert Frost

Yet all men of goodwill have this in common,
that our works, in the end put us to shame, that
always we must begin them afresh, and our sacrifice must be eternally renewed.

Hermann Hesse

My heart bids me do it if I can, and it is a thing
possible to do.

Homer

Jobs

I love work; it fascinates me. I can sit and look at it for hours. I love to keep it by me. The idea of getting rid of it nearly breaks my heart.

Jerome K. Jerome

His weariness is that of the gladiator after the combat; his work was the whitewashing of a corner in a state official's office.

Franz Kafka

Oh, my soul, do not aspire to immortal life, but exhaust the limits of the possible.

Pindar

When you see what some girls marry, you realize how they must hate to work for a living.

H. Rouchard

Hamlet's experience simply could not have happened to a plumber.

George Bernard Shaw

I must be used, built into the solid fabric of life as far as there is any usable brick in me, and thrown aside when I am used up. It is only when I am

being used that I can feel my own existence,
enjoy my own life.

George Bernard Shaw

Nothing is worth doing unless the consequences
may be serious.

George Bernard Shaw

Pursue, keep up with, circle round and round
your life as a dog does with his master's chaise. Do
what you love; know your own bone; gnaw at it,
bury it, unearth it, and gnaw it still.

Henry David Thoreau

Early to rise and early to bed makes a male
healthy and wealthy and dead.

James Thurber

Let us be grateful to Adam. He cut us out of the
blessing of idleness and won for us the curse of
labor.

Mark Twain

*See also ABILITY, ACCOMPLISHMENT, ACHIEVE-
MENT, WORK*

Journeys

Only those who will risk going too far can possibly find out how far one can go.

T. S. Eliot

Travel makes a wise man better but a fool worse.

Thomas Fuller

One may not reach the dawn save by the path of night.

Khalil Gibran

Being in a ship is being in jail, with the chance of being drowned.

Samuel Johnson

Worth seeing? Yes; but not worth going to see.

Samuel Johnson

Whenever I prepare for a journey I prepare as though for death. Should I never return, all is in order. This is what life has taught me.

Katherine Mansfield

A man travels the world over in search of what he needs and returns home to find it.

George Moore

I never travel without my diary. One should always have something sensational to read in the train.

Oscar Wilde

See also *TRAVEL*

Joy

How terrible is man's estate. There is not one of his joys which does not spring out of some form of ignorance.

Honoré de Balzac

On with the dance! Let joy be unconfined.

Lord Byron

There's not a joy the world can give like that it takes away.

Lord Byron

Joy

He chortled in his joy.

Lewis Carroll

You shall have joy, or you shall have power, said
God; you shall not have both.

Ralph Waldo Emerson

Joy, whose hand is ever at his lips, bidding adieu.

John Keats

Weeping may endure for a night, but joy cometh
in the morning.

Psalms 30:5

I found more joy in sorrow than you could find
in joy.

Sara Teasdale

Grief can take care of itself, but to get the full
value of joy you must have somebody to divide it
with.

Mark Twain

Joy is a fruit that Americans eat green.

Amando Zegri

See also FEELINGS, HAPPINESS, PLEASURE

Judgment

It is well, when one is judging a friend, to remember that he is judging you with the same godlike and superior impartiality.

Arnold Bennett

Do not wait for the last judgment. It takes place every day.

Albert Camus

It's Socrates' opinion, and mine too, that it is best judged of heaven not to judge it at all.

Ralph Waldo Emerson

Judge a tree from its fruit, not from the leaves.

Euripides

Don't mind anything that anyone tells you about anyone else. Judge everyone and everything for yourself.

Henry James

Next to sound judgment, diamonds and pearls are the rarest things in the world.

Jean de La Bruyère

Judgment

Everyone complains of his memory, and no one complains of his judgment.

François de La Rochefoucauld

Judge not, that ye be not judged.

Matthew 7:1

We easily enough confess to others as to the advantage of courage, strength, experience, activity, and beauty, but an advantage in judgment we yield to none.

Michel de Montaigne

Men's judgments are a parcel of their fortunes, and things outward do draw the inward quality after them, to suffer all alike.

William Shakespeare: Antony and Cleopatra

Every morning puts a man on trial, and each evening passes judgment.

Roy Smith

One cool judgment is worth a thousand hasty councils. The thing to do is to supply light and not heat.

Woodrow Wilson

Justice

I would rather search for justice than for certainty.

Anonymous

In the Halls of Justice, the only justice is in the halls.

Lenny Bruce

Justice is always violent to the party offending, for every man is innocent in his own eyes.

Daniel Defoe

Justice is too good for some people and not good enough for the rest.

Norman Douglas

Justice is incidental to law and order.

J. Edgar Hoover

Let justice be done, though the heavens fall.

Lord Mansfield

There must be justice for the accuser as well as for the accused.

Robert Mark

Justice

Injustice is relatively easy to bear; what stings is justice.

H. L. Mencken

Be just before you're generous.

Richard Brinsley Sheridan

Justice is like a train that's nearly always late.

Yevgeny Yevtushenko

See also CRIME, LAWS

Kindness

The Turks, a cruel people, who nevertheless are kind to beasts and give alms to dogs and birds.

Francis Bacon

Kindness: a language that the dumb can speak and the deaf can understand.

C. N. Bovee

When kindness has left people, even for a few moments, we become afraid of them, as if their reason had left them.

Willa Cather

Forget injuries; never forget kindness.

Confucius

If you're naturally kind, you attract a lot of people you don't like.

William Feather

Wise sayings often fall on barren ground, but a kind word is never thrown away.

Sir Arthur Helps

Human kindness is like a defective tap, the first gush may be impressive but the stream soon dries up.

P. D. James

To cultivate kindness is a valuable part of the business of life.

Samuel Johnson

Kindness in words creates confidence. Kindness in thinking creates profoundness. Kindness in giving creates love.

Lao-Tse

Kindness

Not always actions show the man: we find,
Who does a kindness is not therefore kind.

Alexander Pope

Do not wait for extraordinary circumstances to do
good; try to use ordinary situations.

Jean Paul Richter

Kind hearts are more than coronets . . .

Alfred Lord Tennyson

One can always be kind to people one cares
nothing about.

Oscar Wilde

That best portion of a good man's life,
His little, nameless, unremembered acts,
Of kindness and of love.

William Wordsworth

See also GOODWILL

Kisses

A kiss is a lovely trick designed by nature to stop
speech when words become superfluous.

Ingrid Bergman

If you are ever in doubt as to whether or not you should kiss a pretty girl, give her the benefit of the doubt.

Thomas Carlyle

What lies lurk in kisses.

Heinrich Heine

When women kiss, it reminds me of prizefighters shaking hands.

H. L. Mencken

Soul meets soul on lover's lips.

Percy Bysshe Shelley

See also LOVE

Knowledge

Crafty men condemn studies, simple men admire them, and wise men use them.

Francis Bacon

I have taken all knowledge to be my province.

Francis Bacon

Knowledge

Knowledge is power.

Francis Bacon

To the small part of ignorance that we arrange and classify, we give the name knowledge.

Ambrose Bierce

More appealing than knowledge itself is the feeling of knowledge.

Daniel J. Boorstin

All that we know is, nothing can be known.

Lord Byron

Human life is limited, but knowledge is limitless. To drive the limited in pursuit of the limitless is fatal, and to presume that one really knows is fatal indeed!

Chuang-Tzu

Although it is dangerous to have too much knowledge of certain subjects, it is still more dangerous to be totally ignorant of them.

Columbat

Seeking to know is only too often learning to doubt.

Antoinette Deshoulières

Where is the Life we have lost in living?
Where is the wisdom we have lost in knowledge?
Where is the knowledge we have lost in information?

T. S. Eliot

Beware of Had I wist.

Fourteenth-century proverb

Know thyself? If I knew myself, I'd run away.

Johann Wolfgang von Goethe

Knowledge is little; to know the right context is much; to know the right spot is everything.

Hugo von Hofmannsthal

The man who is too old to learn was probably always too old to learn.

Henry Hoskins

Knowledge

If a little knowledge is dangerous, where is the man who has so much as to be out of danger?

Thomas Henry Huxley

A man must carry knowledge with him, if he would bring home knowledge.

Samuel Johnson

All knowledge is of itself of some value. There is nothing so minute or inconsiderable that I would not rather know it than not.

Samuel Johnson

Knowledge is of two kinds. We know a subject ourselves, or we know where we can find information upon it.

Samuel Johnson

That observation which is called knowledge of the world will be found much more frequently to make men cunning than good.

Samuel Johnson

Knowledge rests not upon truth alone, but upon error also.

Carl Jung

An extensive knowledge is needful to thinking people—it takes away the heat and fever; and helps, by widening speculation, to ease the Burden of the Mystery.

John Keats

A great deal of learning can be packed into an empty head.

Karl Kraus

All that we know is nothing; we are merely crammed waste-paper baskets unless we are in touch with that which laughs at all our knowing.

D. H. Lawrence

The chief knowledge that a man gets from read-ing books is the knowledge that very few of them are worth reading.

H. L. Mencken

Knowledge is capable of being its own end.

John Henry Cardinal Newman

Those who are slow to know suppose that slow-ness is the essence of knowledge.

Friedrich Wilhelm Nietzsche

Knowledge

The fear of the Lord is the beginning of knowledge . . .

Proverbs 1:7

What others think of us would be of little moment did it not, when known so deeply, tinge what we think of ourselves.

George Santayana

See also BOOKS, EDUCATION, IGNORANCE, WISDOM

Language

For every man there is something in the vocabulary that would stick to him like a second skin. His enemies have only to find it.

Ambrose Bierce

Words have finished flirting; now they are making love.

André Breton

Fancies that broke through language and escaped.

Robert Browning

The coldest word was once a glowing new metaphor.

Thomas Carlyle

The one stream of poetry which is continually flowing is slang.

G. K. Chesterton

How can I tell what I think till I see what I say?

E. M. Forster

The learned fool writes his nonsense in better language than the unlearned, but it is still nonsense.

Benjamin Franklin

Words—so innocent and powerless as they are, as standing in a dictionary, how potent for good and evil they become in the hands of one who knows how to combine them!

Nathaniel Hawthorne

If language had been the creation not of poetry but of logic, we should only have one.

Friedrich Hebbel

Language

If the Romans had been obliged to learn Latin, they would never have found time to conquer the world.

Heinrich Heine

Thanks to words, we have been able to rise above the brutes, and thanks to words, we have sunk to the level of the demons.

Aldous Huxley

My language is the universal whore whom I have to make into a virgin.

L. Kraus

One tongue is sufficient for a woman.

John Milton

Look wise; say nothing, and grunt. Speech was given to conceal thought.

William Osler

Words differently arranged have a different meaning, and meanings differently arranged have a different effect.

Blaise Pascal

The most precious things in speech are pauses.

Ralph Richardson

Words are loaded pistols.

Jean-Paul Sartre

Syllables govern the world.

John Selden

Loquacity storms the ear, but modesty takes the heart.

Robert South

Communication without purpose is artistic masturbation.

Rod Steiger

Man invented language to satisfy his deep need to complain.

Lily Tomlin

Words divide us; action unites us.

Tupamaros

Language

One often makes a remark and only later sees how true it is.

Ludwig Wittgenstein

See also BOOKS, READING, TALK, WORDS

Lateness

Delay always breeds danger, and to protract a great design is often to ruin it.

Miguel de Cervantes

For better than never is late.

Geoffrey Chaucer

Five minutes! Zounds! I have been five minutes too late all my lifetime!

Hannah Cowley

Though last not least.

Edmund Spenser

See also PROCRASTINATION

Laughter

If we may believe our logicians, man is distinguished from all other creatures by the faculty of laughter.

Joseph Addison

A man of parts and fashion is . . . only seen to smile, but never heard to laugh.

Anonymous

I quickly laugh at everything, for fear of having to cry.

Pierre Augustin Caron de Beaumarchais

We laugh but little in our day, but are we less frivolous?

Pierre Jean de Béranger

And if I laugh at any mortal thing,
'Tis that I may not weep.

Lord Byron

Laughter

A laugh, to be joyous, must flow from a joyous heart, for without kindness, there can be no true joy.

Thomas Carlyle

No man who has once heartily and wholly laughed can be altogether irreclaimably bad.

Thomas Carlyle

The most completely lost of all days is the one on which we have not laughed.

Nicolas Chamfort

Laughter is much more important than applause. Applause is almost a duty. Laughter is a reward.

Carol Channing

I am sure that since I have had the full use of my reason nobody has ever heard me laugh.

G. K. Chesterton

Wit ought to be a glorious treat, like caviar. Never spread it about like marmalade.

Sir Noel Coward

How can there be laughter, how can there be
pleasure, when the whole world is burning.

The Dhammapada

Comedy, like sodomy, is an unnatural act.

Marty Feldman

Men show their characters in nothing more
clearly than in what they think laughable.

Johann Wolfgang von Goethe

One half of the world laughs at the other, and
fools are they all.

Baltasar Gracián

Laugh not too much; the witty man laughs last.

George Herbert

We must laugh before we are happy, for fear we
die before we laugh at all.

Jean de La Bruyère

Who laughed there? By God, I think it was I
myself.

Doris Lessing

Laughter

The person who knows how to laugh at himself will never cease to be amused.

Shirley MacLaine

Laugh, if thou art wise.

Martial

Laugh at yourself first before anyone else can.

Elsa Maxwell

Laughter is man's most distinctive emotional expression.

Margaret Mead

Wit has truth in it; wisecracking is simply calisthenics with words.

Dorothy Parker

There is so much to laugh at in this vale of tears.

Hermann Sudermann

Comedy is simply a funny way of being serious.

Peter Ustinov

Laugh, and the world laughs with you;
Weep, and you weep alone.

Ella Wheeler Wilcox

Laughter is not at all a bad beginning for a
friendship, and it is far the best ending for one.

Oscar Wilde

See also HUMOR

Laws

I have forgotten more law than you ever knew,
but allow me to say, I have not forgotten much.

Anonymous

Prisons are built with stones of law, brothels with
bricks of religion.

William Blake

Law and equity are two things which God hath
joined, but which man hath put asunder.

C. C. Colton

Laws

Men would be great criminals did they need as many laws as they make.

Charles John Darling

The law is fair to all. In its fairness for equality, it forbids the rich as well as the poor to beg in the streets and to steal bread.

Anatole France

A jury consists of twelve persons chosen to decide who has the better lawyer.

Robert Frost

Law cannot persuade where it cannot punish.

Thomas Fuller

The English laws punish vice; the Chinese laws do more; they reward virtue.

Oliver Goldsmith

It is the trade of lawyers to question everything, yield nothing, and to talk by the hour.

Thomas Jefferson

Where law ends, tyranny begins.

William Pitt

Wretches hang that jurymen may dine.

Alexander Pope

Government can easily exist without laws, but laws cannot exist without government.

Bertrand Russell

It is criminal to steal a purse, daring to steal a fortune, a mark of greatness to steal a crown. The blame diminishes as the guilt increases.

Friedrich von Schiller

Laws are like cobwebs, which may catch small flies but let wasps and hornets break through.

Jonathan Swift

See also CRIME, JUSTICE

Laziness

Procrastination is suicide on the installment plan.

Anonymous

To loaf is a science; to loaf is to live.

Honoré de Balzac

Laziness

By the street of By-and-By, one arrives at the
house of never.

Miguel de Cervantes

Know the true value of time: snatch, seize, and
enjoy every moment of it. No idleness, no
laziness, no procrastination; never put off till
tomorrow what you can do today.

Lord Chesterfield

We make a mistake if we believe that only the
violent passions like ambition and love can subdue
the others. Laziness for all her languor is nevertheless often mistress; she permeates every aim
and action in life and imperceptibly eats away and
destroys passions and virtues alike.

François de La Rochefoucauld

The really idle man gets nowhere; the perpetually
busy does not get much further.

H. Ogilvie

Failure is not our only punishment for laziness:
there is also the success of others.

Jules Renard

The lazy are always wanting to do something.

Marquis de Vauvenargues

See also IDLENESS, WORK

Learning

. . . Much learning doth make thee mad.

Acts 26:24

Who is wise? He who learns from all men, as it is said, from all my teachers have I gotten an understanding.

Anonymous

What we have to learn to do, we learn by doing.

Aristotle

Doctrine should be such as should make men in love with the lesson and not with the teacher.

Francis Bacon

There is no great concurrence between learning and wisdom.

Francis Bacon

Learning

The life so short, the craft so long to learn.

Geoffrey Chaucer

The University brings out all abilities, including stupidity.

Anton Chekhov

I am always ready to learn although I do not always like being taught.

Winston Churchill

I pay the schoolmaster but 'tis the schoolboys that educate my son.

Ralph Waldo Emerson

Learning makes a good man better and an ill man worse.

Thomas Fuller

I have learned silence from the talkative, toleration from the intolerant, and kindness from the unkind; yet strange, I am ungrateful to those teachers.

Khalil Gibran

Precepts, like fomentations, must be rubbed into us—and with a rough hand too.

Lord Halifax

That which anyone has been long learning unwillingly, he unlearns with proportional eager-ness and haste.

William Hazlitt

In doing we learn.

George Herbert

Learn the fundamentals of the game at your leisure and stick to them. Band-aid remedies never last.

Jack Nicklaus

A little learning is a dangerous thing.

Alexander Pope

Some people will never learn anything, for this reason, because they understand everything too soon.

Alexander Pope

Learning

A tough lesson to learn in life is that not everybody wishes you well.

Dan Rather

Everybody is ignorant, only on different subjects.

Will Rogers

Do you know the difference between education and experience? Education is when you read the fine print, experience is what you get when you don't.

Pete Seeger

According as each has been educated, so he repents of or glories in his actions.

Baruch Spinoza

The first problem for all of us, men and women, is not to learn, but to unlearn.

Gloria Steinem

It is only when we forget all our learning that we begin to know.

Henry David Thoreau

The things we know best are the things we haven't been taught.

Marquis de Vauvenargues

A little learning is not a dangerous thing to one who does not mistake it for a great deal.

William Allen White

In examinations the foolish ask questions that the wise cannot answer.

Oscar Wilde

See also AUTHORS, BOOKS, EDUCATION, LITERATURE, WORDS

Leisure

If you are losing your leisure, look out. You may be losing your soul.

Anonymous

The goal of war is peace; of business, leisure.

Aristotle

Leisure

Overwork, n. A dangerous disorder affecting high public functionaries who want to go fishing.

Ambrose Bierce

The finest amusements are the most pointless ones.

Jacques Chardonne

The most desirable thing in life after health and modest means is leisure with dignity.

Cicero

The wisdom of a learned man cometh by opportunity of leisure; and he that hath little business shall become wise.

Ecclesiastes 38:24

Nothing can exceed the vanity of our existence but the folly of our pursuits.

Oliver Goldsmith

Leisure is the mother of Philosophy.

Thomas Hobbes

Leisure only means a chance to do other jobs that demand attention.

Oliver Wendell Holmes, Jr.

An intellectual improvement arises from leisure.

Samuel Johnson

Most men pursue pleasure with such breathless
haste that they hurry past it.

Søren Kierkegaard

The advantage of leisure is mainly that we
may have the power of choosing our own work,
not certainly that it confers any privilege of idleness.

John Lubbock

The follies which a man regrets most are those
which he didn't commit when he had the opportunity.

Helen Rowland

To be able to fill leisure intelligently is the last
product of civilization.

Bertrand Russell

Generally speaking anybody is more interesting
doing nothing than doing anything.

Gertrude Stein

Leisure

A broad margin of leisure is as beautiful in a man's life as in a book.

Henry David Thoreau

See also IDLENESS, PLEASURE

Letters

If you are in doubt whether to write a letter or not, don't. And the advice applies to many doubts in life besides that of letter writing.

Edward Bulwer-Lytton

. . . not of this letter, but of the spirit; for the letter killeth, but the spirit giveth life.

2 Corinthians 3:6

Chain letters are the postal equivalent of intestinal flu; you get it and pass it along to your friends.

Bob Garfield

When a man sends you an impudent letter, sit right down and give it back to him with interest ten times compounded, and then throw both letters in the wastebasket.

Elbert Hubbard

There are certain people whom one feels almost inclined to urge to hurry up and die so that their letters can be published.

Christopher Morley

The postman is the agent of impolite surprises. Every week we ought to have an hour for receiving letters—and then go and take a bath.

Friedrich Wilhelm Nietzsche

I have made this letter longer than usual because I lack the time to make it short.

Blaise Pascal

Letters give us great lives at their most characteristic, their most glorious, and their most terrible moments. Here history and biography meet.

W. Schuster

Correspondences are like small clothes before the invention of suspenders; it is impossible to keep them up.

Sydney Smith

Letters

I have received no more than one or two letters in my life that were worth the postage.

Henry David Thoreau

See also AUTHORS, BOOKS, WORDS

Liberal

A man who has both feet planted firmly in the air can be safely called a liberal as opposed to the conservative, who has both feet planted in his mouth.

Jacques Barzun

The liberals can understand everything but people who don't understand them.

Lenny Bruce

A liberal is a man who will give away everything he doesn't own.

F. Dane

A liberal is a man too broadminded to take his own side in a quarrel.

Barry Goldwater

Hell hath no fury like a liberal scorned.

Dick Gregory

A Liberal is he who looks forward for his principles of government.

John Stuart Mill

A radical thinks two and two make five. A liberal is more conservative. He knows two and two make four, but he's unhappy about it.

Herbert Prochnow

See also CONSERVATIVE, POLITICS

Liberty

Liberty: one of imagination's most precious possessions.

Ambrose Bierce

They that give up essential liberty to obtain a little temporary safety deserve neither liberty nor safety.

Benjamin Franklin

Liberty

The God who gave us life gave us liberty at the same time.

Thomas Jefferson

We are as great as our belief in human liberty—no greater. And our belief in human liberty is only ours when it is larger than ourselves.

Archibald MacLeish

It is not good to have too much liberty. It is not good to have all one wants.

Blaise Pascal

Liberty means responsibility. That is why most men dread it.

George Bernard Shaw

See also FREEDOM, INDEPENDENCE

Life

✓If life is a grind, use it to sharpen your wits.

Anonymous

Life is a one-way street, and we are not coming back.

Anonymous

298

Life, like a mirror, never gives back more than we put into it.

Anonymous

What then remains but that we still should cry
For being born, and, being born, to die.

Francis Bacon

Life is a long lesson in humility. ✓

Sir James M. Barrie

Every man who refuses to accept the conditions of life sells his soul.

Charles Baudelaire

So this life of man appears for a short space, but of what went before, or what it is to follow, we are utterly ignorant.

The Venerable Bede

Life is short, but it is long enough to ruin any man who wants to be ruined.

Josh Billings

What is life? It is the flash of a firefly in the night. ✓

Blackfeet Indians

Life

For everything that lives is holy; life delights in life.

William Blake

Life is just a bowl of cherries.

Song title by Lou Brown and Ray Henderson

Life is a pure flame, and we live by an invisible sun within us.

Sir Thomas Browne

Where life is more terrible than death, it is then the truest valor to dare to live.

Sir Thomas Browne

Is life worth living? That is a question for an embryo, not a man.

Samuel Butler

✓ Life is one long process of getting tired.

Samuel Butler

Life is the art of drawing sufficient conclusions from insufficient premises.

Samuel Butler

The tragedy of life is not what men suffer, but rather what they miss.

Thomas Carlyle

It's as large as life and twice as natural.

Lewis Carroll

His passions make man live; his wisdom merely makes him last.

Nicolas Chamfort

There is one word which may serve as a rule of practice for all one's life: reciprocity. ✓

Confucius

The river of truth is always splitting up into arms which reunite. Islanded between them, the inhabitants argue for a lifetime as to which is the mainstream.

Cyril Connolly

Life is an incurable disease. ✓

Abraham Cowley

The first half of our life is ruined by our parents, the second half by our children.

Clarence Darrow

Life

Life is too short to be little.

Benjamin Disraeli

When you don't have any money, the problem is food. When you have money, it's sex. When you have both, it's health. If everything is simply jake, then you're frightened of death.

J. P. Donleavy

Only a life lived for others is a life worthwhile.

Albert Einstein

To live remains an art which everyone must learn and which no one can teach.

Havelock Ellis

I want to live my life so that my nights are full of regrets.

F. Scott Fitzgerald

Our lives are but our marches to our graves.

John Fletcher

There is no meaning to life except the meaning man gives his life by the unfolding of his powers.

Eric Fromm

When life does not find a singer to sing her heart, she produces a philosopher to speak her mind.

Khalil Gibran

Life is a joke that's just begun.

Sir William S. Gilbert

Life is made up of interruptions. ✓

Sir William S. Gilbert

A useless life is an early death.

Johann Wolfgang von Goethe

For life I had never cared greatly,
As worth a man's while.

Thomas Hardy

The art of life is to know how to enjoy a little ✓ and to endure much.

William Hazlitt

Everything in excess! To enjoy the flavor of life, take big bites. Moderation is for monks.

Robert Heinlein

Life

✓ You live and learn, or you don't live long.

Robert Heinlein

✓ Life is made up of sobs, sniffles, and smiles, with sniffles predominating.

O. Henry

Life is short, the art long, opportunity fleeting, experience treacherous, judgment difficult.

Hippocrates

✓ I slept and dreamed that life was beauty,
I woke—and found that life was duty.

Ellen Sturgis Hooper

How gaily a man wakes in the morning to watch himself keep on dying.

Henry Hoskins

✓ Life isn't all beer and Skittles . . .

Thomas Hughes

Let your boat of life be light, packed only with what you need—a homely home and simple pleasures, one or two friends worth the name, someone to love and to love you, a cat, a dog, and a

304

pipe or two, enough to eat and enough to wear, and a little more than enough to drink, for thirst is a dangerous thing.

Jerome K. Jerome

. . . all that a man hath will he give for his life.

Job 2:4

Life is barren enough, surely with all her trappings; let us, therefore, be cautious how we strip her.

Samuel Johnson

Welcome O life! I go to encounter for the millionth time the reality of experience and to forge in the smithy of my soul the uncreated conscience of my race.

James Joyce

The Wine of Life keeps oozing drop by drop. The Leaves of Life keep falling one by one.

Omar Khayyám

Life is short. Live it up.

Nikita Khrushchev

Life

Life can only be understood backwards, but it must be lived forwards.

Søren Kierkegaard

There is nothing of which men are so fond, and without care, as life.

Jean de La Bruyère

Life, we learn too late, is in the living, in the tissue of each day and hour.

Stephen Leacock

Life is something to do when you can't get to sleep.

Fran Lebowitz

Life is real! Life is earnest!
And the grave is not its goal;
Dust thou art, to dust returnest,
Was not spoken of the soul.
Tell me not, in mournful numbers,
Life is but an empty dream!
For the soul is dead that slumbers,
And things are not what they seem.

Henry Wadsworth Longfellow

Life's a long headache in a noisy street.

> *John Masefield*

Human existence is always irrational and often painful, but in the last analysis it remains interesting.

> *H. L. Mencken*

My candle burns at both ends;
It will not last the night;
But, ah, my foes, and, oh, my friends—
It gives a lovely light.

> *Edna St. Vincent Millay*

By virtue of being born to humanity, every human being has a right to the development and fulfillment of his potentialities as a human being.

> *Ashley Montague*

Fear not that life shall come to an end but rather fear that it shall never have a beginning.

> *John Henry Cardinal Newman*

If you stop struggling, then you stop life.

> *Howard Newton*

Life

Life is easier than you think; all that is necessary is to accept the impossible, do without the indispensable, and bear the intolerable.

Kathleen Norris

The unexamined life is not worth living.

Plato

Nature has given man no better thing than shortness of life.

Pliny the Elder

Live so you won't be ashamed to sell the family parrot to the town gossip.

Will Rogers

If life were predictable it would cease to be life and be without flavor.

Eleanor Roosevelt

Life is not a spectacle or a feast. It is a predicament.

George Santayana

There is no cure for birth and death save to enjoy the interval.

George Santayana

Life's but a walking shadow, a poor player
That struts and frets his hour upon the stage
And then is heard no more; it is a tale
Told by an idiot, full of sound and fury,
Signifying nothing

William Shakespeare: Macbeth

O gentlemen, the time of life is short!

William Shakespeare: Sonnets

Life in the U.S.A. is a gift.

Bruce Springsteen

To be what we are, and to become what we are
capable of becoming, is the only end of life.

Robert Louis Stevenson

Some go through life getting free rides; others pay
full fare and something extra to take care of the
free riders. Some of the free riders are those who
make an art of "knowing the angles"; others are
rascals; others lazy, but some really need help and
could not ride unless they rode free. I don't spend
much time worrying about the free riders, but I
am a full-fare man, first and last.

David Sutton

Life

I went to the woods because I wished to live
deliberately, to front only the essential facts of life,
and see if I could not learn what it had to teach,
and not, when I came to die, discover that I had
not lived.

Henry David Thoreau

He who only lives wise lives a sad life.

Voltaire

One's real life is so often the life that one does
not lead.

Oscar Wilde

The longer I live, the more keenly I feel that
whatever was good enough for our fathers is not
good enough for us.

Oscar Wilde

A vacuum is a hell of a lot better than some of
the stuff nature replaces it with.

Tennessee Williams

You are the sunshine of my life;
That's why I'll always stay around.

Stevie Wonder

See also AGE, DEATH

Listening

The ear is something we cannot close at will, and we are the poorer for it.

E. Brian

We have two ears and only one tongue so that we would listen more and talk less.

Diogenes

The hearing ear is always found close to the speaking tongue.

Ralph Waldo Emerson

No man would listen to you talk if he didn't know it was his turn next.

Edgar Watson Howe

Listening is the only way to entertain some folks.

Kin (Frank McKinney) Hubbard

The grace of listening is lost if the listener's attention is demanded not as a favor, but as a right.

Pliny the Elder

Listening

Take care what you say before a wall, as you cannot tell who may be behind it.

Sa'di

Give every man thy ear, but few thy voice . . .

William Shakespeare: Hamlet

I know how to listen when clever men are talking. That is the secret of what you call my influence.

Hermann Sudermann

Listening is a very dangerous thing. If one listens, one may be convinced.

Oscar Wilde

Literature

Literature is a luxury; fiction is a necessity.

G. K. Chesterton

That was the chief difference between literature and life. In books, the proportion of exceptional to commonplace people is high; in reality, very low.

Aldous Huxley

The chief glory of every people arises from its authors.

Samuel Johnson

A great literature is chiefly the product of inquiring minds in revolt against the immovable certainties of the nation.

H. L. Mencken

Literature is language charged with meaning.

Ezra Pound

Literature is news that *stays* news.

Ezra Pound

For what are the classics but the noblest recorded thoughts of man? They are the only oracles which are not decayed.

Henry David Thoreau

Literature is the orchestration of platitudes.

Thornton Wilder

See also AUTHORS, BOOKS, LEARNING, READING, WORDS

Loneliness

Separate we come, and separate we go, and this be it known, is all that we know.

Conrad Aiken

People who lead a lonely existence always have something on their minds that they are eager to talk about.

Anton Chekhov

So lonely t'was that God himself
Scarce seemed there to be.

Samuel Taylor Coleridge

A game of pretense; for the essential loneliness is an escape from an inescapable God.

Walter Farrell

Loneliness is the first thing which God's eye nam'd not good.

John Milton

Loneliness . . . is and always has been the central and inevitable experience of every man.

Thomas Wolfe

I wandered lonely as a cloud . . .

William Wordsworth

See also DESPERATION, EMPTINESS, SOLITUDE

Love

Like the measles, love is most dangerous when it comes late in life.

Anonymous

Love is a fan club with only two fans.

Anonymous

Love is the only game that is not called on account of darkness.

Anonymous

When a lover gives, he demands, and much more than he is given.

Anonymous

Oh, love is real enough, you will find it some day but it has one archenemy, and that is life.

Jean Anouilh

Love

Among those whom I like, I can find no common denominator, but among those whom I love, I can: all of them make me laugh.

W. H. Auden

It is impossible to love and be wise.

Francis Bacon

From the moment it is touched, the heart cannot dry up.

Louis Bourdaloue

If thou must love me, let it be for naught,
Except for love's sake only.

Elizabeth Barrett Browning

Love is the business of the idle but the idleness of the busy.

Edward Bulwer-Lytton

But to see her was to love her,
Love but her, and love forever.

Robert Burns

To live is to love; all reason is against it; instinct is for it.

Samuel Butler

Love lasteth as long as the money endureth.

William Caxton

Love in young men, for the most part, is not love but simply sexual desire and its accomplishment is its end.

Miguel de Cervantes

Love is blynd.

Geoffrey Chaucer

She lovede Right fro the firste sighte.

Geoffrey Chaucer

When poverty comes in at doors, love leaps out at windows.

John Clarke

O what a heaven is love! O what a hell!

Thomas Dekker

Love

Love is love's reward.

All mankind loves a lover.

Ralph Waldo Emerson

Next to the coming to a good understanding with
a new mistress, I love a quarrel with an old one.

Sir George Etherege

Perhaps they were right in putting love into
books . . . Perhaps it could not live anywhere else.

William Faulkner

It is an extra dividend when you like the girl
you've fallen in love with.

Clark Gable

A man in love is incomplete until he is married.
Then he is finished.

Zsa Zsa Gabor

Mick Jagger and I just really liked each other a
lot. We talked all night. We had the same views on
nuclear disarmament.

Jerry Hall

Love, and a cough, cannot be hid.

George Herbert

The reduction of the universe to a single being, the expansion of a single being ever to God, this is love.

Victor Hugo

Greater love hath no man than this, that a man lay down his life for his friends.

John 15:13

It is commonly a weak man who marries for love.

Samuel Johnson

Lovers never get tired of each other because they are always talking about themselves.

François de La Rochefoucauld

Love is an egoism of two.

Antoine de La Sale

Love is whatever you can still betray. Betrayal can only happen if you love.

John Le Carre

Love

Of all bodies, the heaviest is the woman who has ceased to love.

Lemontey

I could not love thee, dear, so much,
Loved I not honor more.

Richard Lovelace

It's true that I did get the girl, but then my grand-father always said, "Even a blind chicken finds a few grains of corn now and then."

Lyle Lovett

Come live with me and be my love,
And we will all the pleasures prove . . .

Christopher Marlowe

The head never rules the heart but just becomes its partner in crime.

Michael McLaughlin

Love is the triumph of imagination over intelli-gence.

H. L. Mencken

To be in love is merely to be in a state of perpetual anesthesia—to mistake an ordinary young man for a Greek god or an ordinary young woman for a goddess.

H. L. Mencken

If love and sex are such natural phenomenons how come there are so many books on how to?

Bette Midler

Love is nothing save an insatiate thirst to enjoy a greedily desired object.

Michel de Montaigne

But there's nothing half so sweet in life
As love's young dream

Thomas Moore

The only abnormality is the incapacity to love.

Anaïs Nin

The history of love would be the history of humanity; it would be a beautiful book to write.

Charles Nodier

Love

Love and dignity cannot share the same abode.

Ovid

To be loved, be lovable.

Ovid

Love is composed of so many sensations that something new of it can always be said.

St. Prosper

They love too much that die for love.

John Ray

Love consists in this, that two solitudes protect and touch and greet each other.

Rainer Maria Rilke

To know her was to love her.

Samuel Rogers

To attract men, I wear a perfume called "new car interior."

Rita Rudner

You've got to love something enough to kill it.

Martin Scorsese

There is no love lost between them.

Seventeenth-century expression

...The course of true love never did run smooth.

William Shakespeare: A Midsummer Night's
Dream

No sooner met, but they looked; no sooner
looked but they loved . . .

William Shakespeare: As You Like It

A pair of star-cross'd lovers.

William Shakespeare: Prologue to
Romeo and Juliet

They do not love that do not show their love.

William Shakespeare: The Two Gentlemen of
Verona

The fickleness of the women I love is only
equaled by the infernal constancy of the women
who love me.

George Bernard Shaw

Love is not a matter of counting the years, it's
making the years count.

W. Smith

Love

... Love is strong as death; jealousy is cruel as the grave.

Song of Solomon 8:6

The first duty of love is to listen.

Paul Tillich

To love and to be loved is to feel the sun from both sides.

David Viscott

Will you love me in the good old-fashioned way?
When my hair has all turned gray,
Will you kiss me then and say,
That you love in December as you do in May?

James J. Walker

Let your love be stronger than your hate or anger.
Learn the wisdom of compromise, for it is better
to bend a little than to break.

H. G. Wells

Love conquers all things except poverty and a
toothache.

Mae West

One should always be in love. This is the reason one should never marry.

Oscar Wilde

Women love men for their defects; if men have enough of them, women will forgive them everything, even their gigantic intellects.

Oscar Wilde

Yet each man kills the thing he loves . . .

Oscar Wilde

A man falls in love through his eyes, a woman through her ears.

W. Wyatt

See also FEELINGS, FORGIVING, HATE, KISSES, SEX

Luck

Diligence is the mother of good fortune.

Miguel de Cervantes

Those who mistake their good luck for their merit are inevitably bound for disaster.

J. Christopher Herold

Luck

Little is the luck I've had,
And oh, 'tis comfort small
To think that many another lad
Has had no luck at all.

A. E. Housman

Luck is a dividend of sweat. The more you sweat,
the luckier you get.

Ray A. Kroc

You can take it as understood
That your luck changes only if it's good.

Ogden Nash

Luck affects everything. Let your hook always be
cast in the stream where you least expect there
will be a fish.

Ovid

Well, miss, you'll have a sad husband, you have
such good luck at cards.

Jonathan Swift

See also FATE, OPPORTUNITY

Lying

The two-faced answer or the plain protective lie.

W. H. Auden

Matilda told such dreadful lies,
It made one gasp and stretch one's eyes . . .

Hilaire Belloc

A lie with a purpose is one of the worst kind, and
the most profitable.

Josh Billings

I do not mind lying, but I hate inaccuracy.

Samuel Butler

There are a terrible lot of lies going around the
world, and the worst of it is that they're true.

Winston Churchill

One of the most striking differences between a
cat and a lie is that a cat has only nine lives.

Finley Peter Dunne

Half the truth is often a great lie.

Benjamin Franklin

Lying

Ask me no questions, and I'll tell you no fibs.

Oliver Goldsmith

Why would anyone lie? The truth is always more colorful.

James Hall

The great masses of the people . . . will more easily fall victims to a big lie than to a small one.

Adolf Hitler

She has many tools, but a lie is the handle which fits them all.

Oliver Wendell Holmes

A man had rather have a hundred lies told of him than one truth which he does not wish should be told.

Samuel Johnson

There are times when lying is the most sacred of duties.

Eugène-Marin Labiche

Man is ice to truth and fire to falsehood.

Jean de La Fontaine

It is hard to tell if a man is telling the truth when you know you would lie if you were in his place.

H. L. Mencken

He who does not need to lie is proud of not being a liar.

Friedrich Wilhelm Nietzsche

No one lies so boldly as the man who is indignant.

Friedrich Wilhelm Nietzsche

He that tells a lie to save his credit, wipes his mouth with his sleeve to spare his napkin.

Sir Thomas Overbury

He who tells a lie is not sensible of how great a task he undertakes; for he must be forced to invent twenty more to maintain that one.

Alexander Pope

A liar begins with making falsehood appear like truth and ends with making truth itself appear like falsehood.

William Shenstone

Lying

The cruelest lies are often told in silence.

Robert Louis Stevenson

...A lie which is half a truth is ever the blackest
of lies ...

Alfred Lord Tennyson

There are people who exaggerate so much that
they can't tell the truth without lying.

Mark Twain

The only form of lying that is absolutely beyond
reproach is lying for its own sake.

Oscar Wilde

See also DECEPTION, HYPOCRISY, SINCERITY

Man

Man's inhumanity to man
Makes countless thousands mourn!

Robert Burns

The greatest enemy to man is man, who, by the
devil's instigation, is a wolf, a devil to himself and
others.

Robert Burton

330

So God created man in his own image . . .

Genesis 1:27

Man has never understood how anthropomorphic he is.

Johann Wolfgang von Goethe

Man is the only animal that laughs and weeps; for he is the only animal that is struck with the difference between what things are, and what they ought to be.

William Hazlitt

Man is an intelligence in servitude to his organs.

Aldous Huxley

Man is simply the most formidable of all the beasts of prey, and indeed, the only one that preys systematically on its own species.

William James

I never liked my own species.

Gary Larson

There is no animal in the world so treacherous as man.

Michel de Montaigne

Man

Man that is born of woman is of few days, and full of trouble.

Psalms 90:9

What a piece of work is a man!

William Shakespeare: Hamlet

I wonder men dare trust themselves with men.

William Shakespeare: Timon of Athens

There are many wonderful things in nature, but the most wonderful of all is man.

Sophocles

Man is a rational animal who always loses his temper when he is called upon to act in accordance with the dictates of reason.

Oscar Wilde

See also BACHELORS, BEHAVIOR, CIVILIZATION, HUSBANDS, MARRIAGE, WOMAN

Manners

If a man be gracious, and courteous to strangers, it shows he is a citizen of the world . . .

Francis Bacon

Manners are of more importance than laws. Upon them, in a great measure, the laws depend.

Edmund Burke

A man's natural manner best becomes him.

Cicero

Everyone thinks himself well-bred.

Anthony Ashley Cooper

Evil communications corrupt good manners.

1 Corinthians 15:33

Manners . . . a contrivance of wise men to keep fools at a distance.

Ralph Waldo Emerson

Rudeness is the weak man's imitation of strength.

Eric Hoffer

Every man of any education would rather be called a rascal, than accused of deficiency in the graces.

Samuel Johnson

Civility costs nothing and buys everything.

Lady Mary Wortley Montagu

Manners

Not only each country, but every city, yea and
every vocation hath its own particular decorum.

Michel de Montaigne

... though I am native here
And to the manner born ...

William Shakespeare: Hamlet

Men's evil manners live in brass; their virtues
We write in water.

William Shakespeare: Henry VIII

The great secret is not having bad manners or good
manners or any other particular sort of manners,
but having the same manners for all human souls.

George Bernard Shaw

For a man by nothing is so well betrayed,
As by his manners.

Edmund Spenser

Good breeding consists in concealing how much
we think of ourselves and how little we think of
the other person.

Mark Twain

See also BEHAVIOR, PATIENCE

334

Marriage

If it were not for the presents, an elopement
would be preferable.

George Ade

All comedies are ended by a marriage.

Lord Byron

It is better to marry than to burn.

1 Corinthians 7:9

People marry most happily with their own kind
... [but] at an age where they do not really know
what their own kind is.

Robertson Davies

Marriage is a lottery in which men stake their
liberty, and women their happiness.

De Rieux

The value of marriage is not that adults produce
children but that children produce adults.

Peter De Vries

Marriage

Men marry because they are tired; women because they are curious. Both are disappointed.

Arthur J. Lamb

Marriage, if one will face the truth, is an evil, but a necessary evil.

Menander

It doesn't much signify whom one marries, for one is sure to find next morning that it was someone else.

Samuel Rogers

Marriage is the miracle that transforms the kiss from a pleasure into a duty.

Helen Rowland

Many a good hanging prevents a bad marriage.

William Shakespeare: Twelfth Night

Marriage is popular because it combines the maximum of temptation with the maximum of opportunity.

George Bernard Shaw

Married women are kept women and they are beginning to find it out.

Logan Pearsall Smith

Marriage is kind of frightening, but kind of wonderful, too.

Barbra Streisand

Remember, it's as easy to marry a rich woman as a poor woman.

William Makepeace Thackeray

In married life three is company and two is none.

Oscar Wilde

Assumptions are the termites of relationships.

Henry Winkler

See also *ALIMONY, BACHELORS, DIVORCE, HUSBANDS, MAN, SEX, WIVES, WOMAN*

Memory

There is not any memory with less satisfaction in it than the memory of some temptation we resisted.

James Branch Cabell

Memory

That which is bitter to endure may be sweet to remember.

Thomas Fuller

The true art of memory is the art of attention.

Samuel Johnson

I never forget a face but in your case I'll make an exception.

Groucho Marx

A man's memory may almost become the art of continually varying and misrepresenting his past, according to his interests in the present.

George Santayana

In memory everything seems to happen to music.

Tennessee Williams

Mind

Nothing worth knowing can be understood with the mind.

Woody Allen

I saw the best minds of my generation destroyed
by madness . . .

Allen Ginsberg

You should pray for a sound mind in a sound
body.

Juvenal

What is mind? No matter. What is matter? Never
mind.

Thomas Hewitt Key

A sound mind in a sound body is a short but full
description of a happy state in this world.

John Locke

The mind is its own place, and in itself,
Can make a heaven of hell, a hell of heaven.

John Milton

When the mind's free, the body's delicate.

William Shakespeare: King Lear

An improper mind is a perpetual feast.

Logan Pearsall Smith

Mind

No, what it [my mind] is really most like is a spi-
der's web, insecurely hung on leaves and twigs,
quivering in every wind, and sprinkled with dew-
drops and dead flies.

Logan Pearsall Smith

See also INTELLIGENCE, THOUGHT

Money

If you want to say it with flowers, a single rose
says: "I'm cheap."

Delta Burke

[The rich] are indeed rather possessed by their
memory than possessors.

Robert Burton

They say that knowledge is power. I used to think
so, but I now know that they meant money.

Lord Byron

. . . wine maketh merry: but money answereth all
things.

Ecclesiastes 10:19

Money, wife, is the true fuller's earth for reputations, there is not a spot or a stain but what it can take out.

John Gay

Money is like a sixth sense without which you cannot make a complete use of the other five.

W. Somerset Maugham

But it is pretty to see what money will do.

Samuel Pepys

The love of money is the mother of all evil.

Phocylides

Never invest in anything that eats or needs reparing.

Billy Rose

Money is indeed the most important thing in the world; and all sound and successful personal and national morality should have this fact for its basis.

George Bernard Shaw

The seven deadly sins . . . Food, clothing, firing, rent, taxes, respectability and children. Nothing

Money

can lift those seven millstones from man's neck
but money; and the spirit cannot soar until the
millstones are lifted.

George Bernard Shaw

For the love of money is the root of all evil.

1 Timothy 6:10

See also BUSINESS, DEBT, RICHES, TAXES

Morality

I only know that what is moral is what you feel
good after and what is immoral is what you feel
bad after.

Ernest Hemingway

It is a moral and political axiom that any dishon-
orable act, if performed by oneself, is less immoral
than if performed by someone else who would be
less well-intentioned in his dishonesty.

J. Christopher Herold

The foundation of morality is to have done, once
and for all, with lying.

Thomas Henry Huxley

Veracity is the heart of morality.

Thomas Henry Huxley

They teach the morals of a whore, and the manners of a dancing master.

Samuel Johnson

We know no spectacle so ridiculous as the British public in one of its periodical fits of morality.

Thomas Babington Macaulay

To be a moral man is to obey the traditional maxims of your community without hesitation or discussion.

Charles Sanders Peirce

We have, in fact, two kinds of morality side by side: one which we preach but do not practice, and another which we practice but seldom preach.

Bertrand Russell

Moral indignation is jealousy with a halo.

H. G. Wells

Morality

What is morality in any given time or place? It is what the majority then and there happens to like, and immortality is what they dislike.

Alfred North Whitehead

See also BIBLE, CONSCIENCE, GOD

Music

Music has charms to soothe a savage breast.

William Congreve

It is extraordinary how potent cheap music can be.

Sir Noel Coward

It will be generally admitted that Beethoven's Fifth Symphony is the most sublime noise that has ever penetrated into the ear of man.

E. M. Forster

Opera is when a guy gets stabbed in the back and instead of bleeding, he sings.

Ed Gardner

Most people get into bands for three very simple rock-and-roll reasons: to get laid, to get fame, and to get rich.

Bob Geldof

I want to be in a musical movie like *Evita,* but with good music.

Elton John

And the night shall be filled with music,
And the cares that infest the day,
Shall fold their tents like the Arabs,
And as silently steal away.

Henry Wadsworth Longfellow

There are only two kinds of music; German music and bad music.

H. L. Mencken

Such sweet compulsion doth in music lie.

John Milton

As some to church repair,
Not for the doctrine, but the music there.

Alexander Pope

Music

Music oft hath such a charm
To make bad good, and good provoke to harm.

William Shakespeare: Measure for Measure

If music be the food of love, play on . . .

William Shakespeare: Twelfth Night

Hell is full of musical amateurs. Music is the
brandy of the damned.

George Bernard Shaw

Wagner's music is better than it sounds.

Mark Twain

See also THE ARTS, CREATIVITY

Neighbor

You're never quite sure how you feel about a
neighbor until a "For Sale" sign suddenly appears
in front of his house.

O. A. Battista

It is discouraging to try to be a good neighbor in
a bad neighborhood.

William R. Castle

It is good manners which make the excellence of a neighborhood.

Confucius

Good fences make good neighbors.

Robert Frost

Love your neighbor, yet pull not down your hedge.

George Herbert

Your neighbor is the man who needs you.

Elbert Hubbard

The impersonal hand of government can never replace the helping hand of a neighbor.

Hubert H. Humphrey

Nothing makes you more tolerant of a neighbor's noisy party than being there.

Franklin P. Jones

Thou shalt love thy neighbour as thyself.

Leviticus 19:18

Neighbor

The crop always seems better in our neighbor's field, and our neighbor's cow gives more milk.

Ovid

Get acquainted with your neighbor; you might like him.

Father H. B. Tierney

Living next to you is in some ways like sleeping with an elephant. No matter how friendly and even-tempered is the beast, one is affected by every twitch and grunt.

Pierre Elliot Trudeau

What would I do without my neighbor when the grocery store is closed? One-fourth cup of sugar borrowed at a convenient time has saved many a pie, contributed to many a festivity.

Dariel Walsh

Opinions

The more unpopular an opinion is, the more necessary is it that the holder should be somewhat punctilious in his observance of conventionalities generally.

Samuel Butler

The public buys its opinions as it buys its meat, or takes in its milk, on the principle that it is cheaper to do this than to keep a cow. So it is, but the milk is more likely to be watered.

Samuel Butler

Men who borrow their opinions can never repay their debts.

Lord Halifax

The foolish and the dead alone never change their opinion.

James Russell Lowell

. . . Opinion in good men is but knowledge in the making.

John Milton

Some praise at morning what they blame at night, But always think the last opinion right.

Alexander Pope

Opinion is something wherein I go about to give reasons why all the world should think as I think.

John Selden

Opinions

Opinion is ultimately determined by the feelings, and not by the intellect.

Herbert Spencer

See also CONVICTIONS

Opportunity

A wise man will make more opportunities than he finds.

Francis Bacon

Opportunity. A favorable occasion for grasping a disappointment.

Ambrose Bierce

No great man ever complains of want of opportunity.

Ralph Waldo Emerson

Time's ancient bawd, Opportunity.

William Rowley

Luck is what happens when preparation meets opportunity.

Darrell Royal

Who seeks, and will not take when once 'tis offer'd,
Shall never find it more.

William Shakespeare: Antony and Cleopatra

We must take the current when it serves,
Or lose our ventures.

William Shakespeare: Julius Caesar

Wealth in modern societies is distributed according to opportunity; and while opportunity depends partly upon talent and energy, it depends still more upon birth, social position, access to education and inherited wealth; in a word, upon property.

Richard H. Tawney

See also FATE, LUCK

Optimism

The optimist proclaims that we live in the best of all possible worlds; and the pessimist fears this is true.

James Branch Cabell

A pessimist is a man who thinks all women are bad. An optimist is a man who hopes they are.

Chauncey Depew

351

Optimism

Optimism is a kind of heart stimulant—the digitalis of failure.

Elbert Hubbard

Two men look out through the same bars;
One sees the mud, and one the stars.

Frederick Langbridge

An optimist is a guy
that has never had
much experience.

Don Marquis

An optimist builds castles in the air. A pessimist is one who builds dungeons in the same place.

Walter Winchell

See also DREAMS, HOPE

Originality

I think one of the reasons I am popular again is because I'm wearing a tie. You have to be different.

Tony Bennett

For I fear I have nothing original in me
Excepting Original Sin.

Thomas Campbell

In order to be irreplaceable, one must always be
different.

Coco Chanel

There is nothing mysterious about originality,
nothing fantastic. Originality is merely the step
beyond.

L. Danze

He has left off reading altogether, to the great
improvement of his originality.

Charles Lamb

Original thought is like original sin: both
happened before you were born to people you
could not have possibly met.

Fran Lebowitz

All good things which exist are the fruits of
originality.

John Stuart Mill

Originality

Originality does not consist in saying what no one has ever said before, but in saying exactly what you think yourself.

J. F. Stephen

See also CREATIVITY, CONFORMITY, INDIVIDUALISM

Parents

Diogenes struck the father when the son swore.

Robert Burton

You are the bows from which your children are as living arrows sent forth.

Khalil Gibran

There must always be a struggle between a father and son, while one aims at power and the other at independence.

Samuel Johnson

Greatness of name in the father oft-times overwhelms the son; they stand too near one another. The shadow kills the growth: so much, that we see the grandchild come more and oftener to be heir of the first.

Ben Jonson

Like father, like son.

William Langland

The best academy, a mother's knee.

James Russell Lowell

Oh, what a tangled web do parents weave
When they think that their children are naïve.

Ogden Nash

Experts say you should never hit your children in
anger. When is a good time? When you're feeling
festive?

Roseanne

Parents like the idea of kids, they just don't like
their kids.

Morley Safer

I tell you there's a wall ten feet thick and ten
miles high between parent and child.

George Bernard Shaw

Happy is the child whose father goes to the devil.

Sixteenth-century proverb

Parents

Trust yourself. You know more than you think you do.

Benjamin Spock

What good mothers and fathers instinctively feel like doing for their babies is usually best after all.

Benjamin Spock

Parenthood remains the greatest single preserve of the amateur.

Alvin Toffler

Parents must get across the idea that "I love you always, but sometimes I do not love your behavior."

Amy Vanderbilt

The hand that rocks the cradle is the hand that rules the world.

William Ross Wallace

Fathers should be neither seen nor heard. That is the only proper basis for family life.

Oscar Wilde

Mom worship has got completely out of hand.

Philip Wylie

See also ANCESTRY, CHILDREN, FAMILY

Patience

Lord, grant me patience, and I want it right now.

Anonymous

Patience, n. A minor form of despair, disguised as a virtue.

Ambrose Bierce

Everything comes if a man will only wait.

Benjamin Disraeli

Beware the fury of a patient man.

John Dryden

Possess your soul with patience.

John Dryden

Patience, that blending of moral courage with physical timidity.

Thomas Hardy

Patience

All things come round to him who will but wait.

Henry Wadsworth Longfellow

Learn to labour and to wait.

Henry Wadsworth Longfellow

Patience, the beggar's virtue.

Philip Massinger

They also serve who only stand and wait.

John Milton

There is a point when patience ceases to be a virtue.

Thomas Morton

You heavens, give me that patience, patience I need.

William Shakespeare: King Lear

See also CHARACTER, MANNERS

Peace

Give peace in our time, O Lord.

The Book of Common Prayer

Peace with honor. I believe it is peace for our
time . . .

Neville Chamberlain

The most advantageous peace is better than the
most just war.

Erasmus

You cannot shake hands with a clenched fist.

Indira Gandhi

If you cannot find peace within yourself, you will
never find it anywhere else.

Marvin Gaye

Anything for a quiet life.

Thomas Heywood

Peace at any price.

Alphonse de Lamartine

Glory to God in the highest, and on earth peace,
goodwill toward men.

Luke 2:14

Peace

Peace hath her victories
No less renowned than war

John Milton

The peace of God, which passeth all understanding . . .

Philippians 4:7

Peace begins just where ambition ends.

Edward Young

See also CONTENTMENT, WAR

Pleasure

Pleasure's a sin, and sometimes sin's a pleasure.

Lord Byron

Pleasure is the absence of pain.

Cicero

Instant gratification is not soon enough.

Carrie Fisher

The honest man takes pains and then enjoys pleasures; the knave takes pleasure, and then suffers pain.

Benjamin Franklin

A life of pleasure is the most unpleasant thing in the world.

Oliver Goldsmith

The last pleasure in life is the sense of discharging our duty.

William Hazlitt

I can sympathize with people's pains but not with their pleasures. There is something curiously boring about somebody else's happiness.

Aldous Huxley

Having now nobody to please, I am little pleased.

Samuel Johnson

Pleasure is very seldom found where it is sought.

Samuel Johnson

Pleasure

Life would be tolerable were it not for its amusements.

Sir George Cornewall Lewis

There is no such thing as pure pleasure; some anxiety always goes with it.

Ovid

Pleasure is nothing else but the intermission of pain.

John Selden

Life would be very pleasant if it were not for its enjoyments.

Robert Smith Surtees

The true pleasure of life is to live with your inferiors.

William Makepeace Thackeray

Simple pleasures are the last refuge of the complex.

Oscar Wilde

All the things I really like to do are either immoral, illegal, or fattening.

Alexander Woollcott

See also HAPPINESS, JOY, LEISURE

Politics

Politics makes estranged bedfellows.

Goodman Ace

All political parties die at last of swallowing their own lies.

John Arbuthnot

Politics. The conduct of public affairs for private advantage.

Ambrose Bierce

Have you ever seen a candidate talking to a rich person on TV?

Art Buchwald

In Mexico an air conditioner is called a politician because it makes a lot of noise but doesn't work very well.

Len Deighton

Politics

In politics there is no honor.

Benjamin Disraeli

I think politics is the instrument of the devil.

Bob Dylan

Politics are too serious a matter to be left to the politicians.

Charles de Gaulle

You cannot adopt politics as a profession and remain honest.

Louis McHenry Howe

Politics is the enemy of the imagination.

Ian MacEwen

Being in politics is like being a football coach . . . smart enough to know the game and stupid enough to think it is important.

Eugene McCarthy

The whole aim of practical politics is to keep the populace alarmed (and hence clamorous to be led to safety) by an endless series of hobgoblins.

H. L. Mencken

Politics is just like show business, you have a hell of an opening, coast for a while, and then have a hell of a close.

Ronald Reagan

Politics is supposed to be the second oldest profession. I have come to realize it bears a very close resemblance to the first.

Ronald Reagan

All politics are based on the indifference of the majority.

James Reston

In politics if you want anything said, ask a man. If you want anything done, ask a woman.

Margaret Thatcher

Politics makes strange bedfellows.

Charles Dudley Warner

See also CONSERVATIVE, GOVERNMENT, LIBERAL

Poverty

There is no man so poor but what he can afford to keep one dog.

Josh Billings

Poverty is the Muse's patrimony.

Robert Burton

To be poor and independent is very nearly an impossibility.

William Cobbett

There is no virtue that poverty destroyeth not.

John Florio

Poverty is not a shame, but the being ashamed of it is.

Thomas Fuller

Poverty is the openmouthed relentless hell which yawns beneath civilized society.

Henry George

It's no disgrace t'be poor, but it might as well be.

Kin (Frank McKinney) Hubbard

In the prospect of poverty there is nothing but gloom and melancholy; the mind and body suffer together; its miseries bring no alleviations; it is a state in which every virtue is obscured, and in which cheerfulness is insensibility, and dejection sullenness, of which the hardships are without honor, and the labors without reward.

Samuel Johnson

Poverty is a great enemy to human happiness.

Samuel Johnson

Poverty is a soft pedal upon all branches of human activity, not excepting the spiritual.

H. L. Mencken

I've never been poor, only broke. Being poor is a frame of mind. Being broke is only a temporary situation.

Mike Todd

See also DEBT, RICHES

Power

Power tends to corrupt and absolute power corrupts absolutely.

Lord Acton

Power, like lightning, injures before its warning.

Pedro Calderón de la Barca

It takes tremendous discipline to control the influence, the power you have over other people's lives.

Clint Eastwood

Respect your efforts, respect yourself. Self-respect leads to self-discipline. When you have both firmly under your belt, that's real power.

Clint Eastwood

The only prize much cared for by the powerful is power.

Oliver Wendell Holmes

Power is always gradually stealing away from the many to the few, because the few are more vigilant and consistent.

Samuel Johnson

Wherever I found a living creature, there I found
the will to power.

Friedrich Wilhelm Nietzsche

Unlimited power is apt to corrupt the minds of
those who possess it . . .

William Pitt

Power, like a desolating pestilence,
Pollutes whate'er it touches . . .

Percy Bysshe Shelley

Power does not corrupt. Fear corrupts, perhaps
the fear of a loss of power.

John Steinbeck

The lust for power, for dominating others,
inflames the heart more than any other passion.

Tacitus

They who are in highest places, and have the
most power, have the least liberty, because they are
most observed.

John Tillotson

Praise

The advantage of doing one's praising for oneself is that one can lay it on so thick and exactly in the right places.

Samuel Butler

Praises to the unworthy are felt by ardent minds as robberies of the deserving.

Samuel Taylor Coleridge

Good men hate those who praise them if they praise them too much.

Euripides

The praise of a fool is more harmful than his blame.

Jean Pierre Claris de Florian

Faint Praise is Disparagement.

Thomas Fuller

He that praiseth publickly, will slander privately.

Thomas Fuller

Our heartiest praise is usually reserved for our admirers.

François de La Rochefoucauld

The refusal of praise is a wish to be praised twice.

François de La Rochefoucauld

Usually we praise only to be praised.

François de La Rochefoucauld

Damn with faint praise, assent with civil leer . . .

Alexander Pope

Fondly we think we honor merit then,
When we but praise ourselves in other men.

Alexander Pope

I will praise any man that will praise me.

William Shakespeare: Antony and Cleopatra

Prejudice

If we were to wake up some morning and find
that everyone was the same race, creed and color,

we would find some other causes for prejudice by noon.

Senator George Aiken

Nothing is more dangerous than an idea, when it's the only one we have.

Alain

Prejudice saves a lot of time, because you can form an opinion without the facts.

Anonymous

There are only two ways to be unprejudiced and impartial. One is to be completely ignorant. The other is to be completely indifferent. Bias and prejudice are attitudes to be kept in hand, not attitudes to be avoided.

Charles Curates

Prejudices are the props of civilization.

André Gide

If a guy's got it, let him give it. I'm selling music, not prejudice.

Benny Goodman

Prejudice is never easy unless it can pass itself off for reason.

William Hazlitt

Prejudice is the child of ignorance.

William Hazlitt

Prejudice is a raft onto which the shipwrecked mind clambers and paddles to safety.

Ben Hecht

The mind of a bigot is like the pupil of an eye; the more light you pour into it, the more it will contract.

Oliver Wendell Holmes

Prejudice not founded on reason cannot be removed by argument.

Samuel Johnson

One may no more live in the world without picking up the moral prejudices of the world, than one would be able to go to hell without perspiring.

H. L. Mencken

Prejudice

Nothing is so firmly believed as what is least known.

Michel de Montaigne

All looks yellow to a jaundiced eye.

Alexander Pope

Most men, when they think they are thinking, are merely rearranging their prejudices.

Knute Rockne

We must not allow prejudice to become a barrier to the full and effective use of our greatest national resources—the talents of our people.

Lynn A. Townsend

If we believe absurdities, we shall commit atrocities.

Voltaire

Prejudice is an opinion without judgment.

Voltaire

Prejudice is the reasoning of the stupid.

Voltaire

Passion and prejudice govern the world.

John Wesley

See also AFRICAN-AMERICANS, CONVICTIONS,
RACE and RACISM

Procrastination

Never do today what you can do tomorrow.
Something may occur to make you regret your
premature action.

Aaron Burr

Procrastination is opportunity's natural assassin.

Victor Kiam

Procrastination is the art of keeping up with
yesterday.

Don Marquis

Procrastination is the thief of time.

Edward Young

See also LATENESS

Race and Racism

It's a great shock at the age of five or six to find that in a world of Gary Coopers—you are the Indian.

James Baldwin

Whites must be made to realize that they are only human, not superior. Same with blacks. They must be made to realize that they are also human, not inferior.

Stephen Biko

Racism? But isn't it only a form of misanthropy?

Joseph Brodsky

There are only two races on this planet—the intelligent and the stupid.

John Fowles

As the global expansion of Indian and Chinese restaurants suggests, xenophobia is directed against foreign people, not foreign cultural imports.

Eric Hobsbawm

Race and Racism

No one has been barred on account of his race from fighting or dying for America—there are no "white" or "colored" signs on the foxholes or graveyards of battle.

John F. Kennedy

This blasphemy attributes to God that which is of the devil.

Martin Luther King, Jr.

People shouldn't be treated like animals. They aren't that valuable.

P. J. O'Rourke

There's no such thing as race and barely such a thing as an ethnic group. If we were dogs, we'd be the same breed.

P. J. O'Rourke

Racism is a disease. See a doctor!

English graffiti as reported by Paul Theroux

See also AFRICAN-AMERICANS, PREJUDICE

Reading

Read, mark, learn, and inwardly digest.

The Book of Common Prayer

Let blockheads read what blockheads write.

Lord Chesterfield

A man ought to read just as inclination leads him;
for what he reads as a task will do him little good.

Samuel Johnson

He has left off reading altogether, to the great
improvement of his originality.

Charles Lamb

Reading furnishes our mind only with materials
of knowledge; it is thinking makes what we read
ours.

John Locke

I'm quite illiterate, but I read a lot.

J. D. Salinger

Language is the soul of intellect, and reading is
the essential process by which that intellect is cul-

tivated beyond the commonplace experiences of everyday life.

Charles Scribner, Jr.

People say that life is the thing, but I prefer reading.

Logan Pearsall Smith

Then I thought of reading—the nice and subtle happiness of reading . . . this joy not dulled by Age, this polite and unpunishable vice, this selfish, serene, life-long intoxication.

Logan Pearsall Smith

There is an implied contract between author and reader.

William Wordsworth

See also AUTHORS, BOOKS, EDUCATION, LANGUAGE, LITERATURE, WORDS

Reality

Melancholy and remorse form the deep leaden keel which enables us to sail into the wind of reality.

Cyril Connolly

Reality

. . . human kind
cannot bear very much reality.

T. S. Eliot

Chaos is the score upon which reality is written.

Henry Miller

Man . . . will debauch himself with ideas, he will
reduce himself to a shadow if for only one second
of his life he can close his eyes to the hideousness
of reality.

Henry Miller

There is nothing in words, believe what is before
your eyes.

Ovid

Real life is, to most men, a long second-best, a
perpetual compromise between the ideal and the
possible.

Bertrand Russell

The test which the mind applies to every question must be the test of reality; of validity
measured through reason by reality. And yet the

dogmatists call those weak who choose the harder, the more rigorous way.

Dorothy Thompson

Reason

As reason is a Rebel unto Faith, so Passion unto Reason.

Sir Thomas Browne

It's common for men to give pretended Reasons instead of one real one.

Benjamin Franklin

The heart has its reasons which reason cannot know.

Blaise Pascal

The man who listens to Reason is lost; Reason enslaves all whose minds are not strong enough to master her.

George Bernard Shaw

See also IDEAS, INSANITY, THOUGHT

Religion

Politics and church are the same thing. They keep the people in ignorance.

Anonymous

You have to be very religious to change your religion.

Anonymous

As the caterpillar chooses the fairest leaves to lay her eggs on, so the priest lays his curse on the fairest joys.

William Blake

Wandering in a forest late at night, I have only a faint light to guide me. A stranger appears and says to me, "My friend, you should blow out your candle in order to find your way more clearly." This stranger is a theologian.

Denis Diderot

I like the silent church before the service begins better than any preaching.

Ralph Waldo Emerson

The religions we call false were once true.

Ralph Waldo Emerson

A religion, even if it calls itself the religion of
love, must be hard and unloving to those who do
not belong to it.

Sigmund Freud

The trees reflected in the river—they are unconscious of a spiritual world so near them. So
are we.

Nathaniel Hawthorne

One thing is pretty obvious in these days. If the
clergy went on strike, society would soon learn to
live without them.

Jules Jacques

The true way goes over a rope which is not
stretched at any great height but just above the
ground. It seems more designed to make people
stumble than to be walked upon.

Franz Kafka

When the missionaries arrived, the Africans had
the land, and the missionaries had the Bible; they

taught us to pray with our eyes closed. When we opened them, they had the land, and we had the Bible.

Jomo Kenyatta

A pious man is one who would be an atheist if the king were.

Jean de La Bruyère

To what excesses will men not go for the sake of a religion in which they believe so little and which they practice so imperfectly!

Jean de La Bruyère

Religion is built on humility; honor on pride. How to reconcile them must be left to wiser heads than mine.

Tommy Manville

It were better to be of no church than to be bitter for any.

William Penn

All religions will pass, but this will remain: simply sitting in a chair and looking in the distance.

Vasili Vasilievich Rozanov

All religions promise a reward for excellence of the will or heart, but none for excellence of the head or understanding.

Arthur Schopenhauer

A man is accepted into a church for what he believes and he is turned out for what he knows.

Mark Twain

See also AFTERLIFE, CHRISTIANITY, FAITH, GOD

Reputation

The easiest way to get a reputation is to go outside the fold, shout around for a few years as a violent atheist or a dangerous radical, and then crawl back to the shelter.

F. Scott Fitzgerald

He that hath the name to be an early riser may sleep till noon.

James Howell

Be it true or false, what is said about men often has as much influence upon their lives, and especially upon their destinies, as what they do.

Victor Hugo

Reputation

Woe unto you, when all men shall speak well of you!

Luke 6:26

Perhaps the most valuable of all human possessions, next to an aloof and sniffish air, is the reputation of being well-to-do.

H. L. Mencken

Revenge

A man that studieth revenge keeps his own wounds green.

Francis Bacon

Sweet is revenge—especially to women.

Lord Byron

Revenge is profitable, gratitude is expensive.

Edward Gibbon

O revenge, how sweet thou art!

Ben Jonson

Revenge is sweet.

Thomas Southerne

See also HATE

Riches

It isn't necessary to be rich and famous to be happy. It's only necessary to be rich.

Alan Alda

Put in its proper place, money is not man's enemy, not his undoing, nor his master. It is his servant, and it must be made to serve him well.

Henry C. Alexander

Money is sweet balm.

Arab proverb

The ways to enrich are many, and most of them foul.

Francis Bacon

Ready money is Aladdin's lamp.

Lord Byron

Riches

The man who dies rich . . . dies disgraced.

Andrew Carnegie

Even the blind can see money.

Chinese proverb

Riches have wings, and grandeur is a dream.

William Cowper

If you have no money, be polite.

Danish proverb

There is pain in getting, care in keeping, and grief
in losing riches.

Thomas Draxe

The art of getting rich consists not in industry,
much less in savings, but in a better order, in
timeliness, in being at the right spot.

Ralph Waldo Emerson

A rich man is nothing but a poor man with
money.

W. C. Fields

Let me tell you about the very rich. They are different from you and me. They possess and enjoy early, and it does something to them, makes them feel soft where we are hard, and cynical where we are trustful, in a way, that, unless you were born rich, it is very difficult to understand.

F. Scott Fitzgerald

No man ever had enough money.

Gypsy proverb

The rich who are unhappy are worse off than the poor who are unhappy; for the poor, at least, cling to the hopeful delusion that more money would solve their problems—but the rich know better.

Sydney J. Harris

Make money, money by fair means if you can, if not, by any means money.

Horace

Virtue, glory, honor, all things human and divine, are slaves to riches.

Horace

Riches

Money has no ears, but it hears.

Japanese proverb

I have not observed men's honesty to increase
with their riches.

Thomas Jefferson

Riches are chiefly good because they give us
time.

Charles Lamb

I've been rich, and I've been poor. And believe
me, rich is better.

Joe E. Lewis

It is easier for a camel to go through the eye of a
needle than for a rich man to enter into the kingdom of God.

Matthew 19:24

For all you can hold in your cold dead hand
Is what you have given away

Joaquin Miller

He that trusteth in his riches shall fall.

Proverbs 24:28

Right

People who are hard, grasping and always ready to take advantage of their neighbors, become very rich . . .

George Bernard Shaw

You can never be too thin or too rich.

Wallis Warfield Simpson

No man is rich enough to buy back his past.

Oscar Wilde

The embarrassment of riches.

Voltaire

See also MONEY, POVERTY, SUCCESS

Right

God's in his heaven
All's right with the world!

Robert Browning

The need to be right—the sign of a grumble mind.

Albert Camus

Right

I would rather be right than be President.

Henry Clay

A fool must now and then be right, by chance.

William Cowper

When all goes right and nothing goes wrong?
And isn't your life extremely flat
With nothing whatever to grumble at.

Sir William S. Gilbert

When you are right, you cannot be too radical.
When you are wrong, you cannot be too conservative.

Martin Luther King, Jr.

Let us have faith that right makes might . . .

Abraham Lincoln

Always do right. This will gratify some people,
and astonish the rest.

Mark Twain

See also VIRTUE

Security

The most secure individual in our society is a prisoner serving a life sentence.

Senator Joseph Ball

The tendency is to be broadminded about other people's security.

Aristide Briand

Too many people are thinking of security instead of opportunity. They seem more afraid of life than death.

James Byrnes

If all that Americans want is security they can go to prison.

Dwight D. Eisenhower

Distrust and caution are the parents of security.

Benjamin Franklin

Some sense of security is necessary to happy or healthful living, but you cannot get it by refusing to take chances any more than a country can get it by living behind walls.

Lawrence Gould

Security

It is much more secure to be feared than to be loved.

Niccolò Machiavelli

Only those means of security are good, are certain, are lasting, that depend on yourself and your own vigor.

Niccolò Machiavelli

Self

Who finds himself, loses his misery!

Matthew Arnold

It is a poor center of a man's actions, himself.

Francis Bacon

He is a poor creature who does not believe himself to be better than the world. No matter how ill we may be, or how low we may have fallen, we would not change identity with any other person. Hence our self-conceit sustains and always must sustain us till death takes us and our conceit together so that we need no more sustaining.

Samuel Butler

Self-preservation is the first law of nature.

Samuel Butler

To know oneself, one should assert oneself.

Albert Camus

Who in the world am I? Ah, that's the great puzzle.

Lewis Carroll

A man is least known to himself.

Cicero

Know thyself.

Inscribed on the temple at Delphi

Trust thyself; every heart vibrates to that iron string.

Ralph Waldo Emerson

We reproach people for talking about themselves; but it is the subject they treat best.

Anatole France

We talk little, if we do not talk about ourselves.

William Hazlitt

Self

Self-confidence is the first requisite to great undertakings.

Samuel Johnson

He that is giddy thinks the world turns round.

William Shakespeare: The Taming of the Shrew

I have said that the soul is not more than the
body,
And I have said that the body is not more than
the soul,
And nothing, not God, is greater to one than
one's self is.

Walt Whitman

See also BEHAVIOR, EGO

Sex

Who says two sexes aren't enough?

Samuel Hoffenstein

Sex was invented in America in the 60s. Before
that, it didn't exist.

Robert Horst

'Tis the Devil inspires this evanescent ardor, in order to divert the parties from prayer.

Martin Luther

All this humorless document (the *Kinsey Report*) really proves is; (a) that all men lie when they are asked about their adventures in amour and (b) that pedagogues are singularly naïve and credulous creatures.

H. L. Mencken

There is no greater nor keener pleasure than that of bodily love—and none which is more irrational.

Plato

When we will, they won't; when we don't want to, they want to exceedingly.

Terence

Women, observing that her mate went out of his way to make himself entertaining, rightly surmised that sex had something to do with it. From that she logically concluded that sex was recreational rather than procreational.

James Thurber and E. B. White

See also CHASTITY, LOVE, MARRIAGE

Silence

Silence is one of the hardest things to refute.

Josh Billings

"Speech is silvern, Silence is golden"; or, as I might rather express it, speech is of time, silence is of eternity.

Thomas Carlyle

Silence is one great art of conversation.

William Hazlitt

There is an eloquent silence: it serves sometimes to approve, sometimes to condemn; there is a mocking silence, there is a respectful silence.

François de La Rochefoucauld

There is no reply so sharp as silent contempt.

Michel de Montaigne

The silence often of pure innocence
Persuades when speaking fails.

William Shakespeare: The Winter's Tale

The world would be happier if men had the same capacity to be silent that they have to speak.

Baruch Spinoza

Silence may be as variously shaded as speech.

Edith Wharton

See also CONVERSATION, TALK

Sincerity

Love of talking about ourselves and displaying our faults in the light of which we wish them to be seen is the chief element in our sincerity.

François de La Rochefoucauld

It is dangerous to be sincere unless you are also stupid.

George Bernard Shaw

Be suspicious of your sincerity when you are the advocate of that upon which your livelihood depends.

John Lancaster Spalding

Sincerity

A little sincerity is a dangerous thing, and a great deal of it is absolutely fatal.

Oscar Wilde

See also DECEPTION, HYPOCRISY, LYING

Solitude

Whoever is delighted in solitude is either a wild beast or a god.

Francis Bacon

Solitude: A good place to visit, but a poor place to stay.

Josh Billings

A man, alone, is either a saint or a devil.

Robert Burton

Solitude: A luxury of the rich.

Albert Camus

It is not good that the man should be alone ...

Genesis 2:18

People who cannot bear to be alone are generally the worst company.

Albert Guinon

A solitude is the audience chamber of God.

Walter Savage Landor

Who can enjoy alone?

John Milton

Man cannot long survive without air, water, and sleep. Next in importance comes food. And close on its heels, solitude.

Thomas Szasz

I never found the companion that was so companionable as solitude.

Henry David Thoreau

The happiest of all lives is a busy solitude.

Voltaire

See also LONELINESS

Sorrow

You cannot prevent the birds of sorrow from flying over your head, but you can prevent them from building nests in your hair.

Chinese proverb

This is my last message to you: in sorrow seek happiness.

Feodor Dostoyevsky

... In sorrow thou shalt bring forth children ...

Genesis 3:16

Sorrows are like thunderclouds. Far off they look black, but directly over us is merely gray.

Jean Paul Richter

A countenance more in sorrow than in anger.

William Shakespeare: Hamlet

When sorrows come, they come not single spies, But in battalions.

William Shakespeare: Hamlet

Some natural sorrow, loss, or pain,
That has been, and may be again.

William Wordsworth

See also FEELINGS, GRIEF, SUFFERING

Success

The toughest thing about success is that you've got to keep on being a success. Talent is only a starting point in this business.

Irving Berlin

Nothing succeeds like success.

Alexandre Dumas, père

Success has ruined many a man.

Benjamin Franklin

Success—"the bitch-goddess Success," in William James's phrase—demands strange sacrifices from those who worship her.

Aldous Huxley

Success

If winning isn't everything, why do they keep score?

Vince Lombardi

Winning is a habit. Unfortunately, so is losing.

Vince Lombardi

Success or failure lies in conformity to the times.

Niccolò Machiavelli

I have always observed that to succeed in the world one should seem a fool, but be wise.

Baron de Montesquieu

Let me tell you the secret that has led me to my goal. My strength lies solely in my tenacity.

Louis Pasteur

How can you say my life is not a success? Have I not for more than sixty years got enough to eat and escaped being eaten?

Logan Pearsall Smith

All you need in this life is ignorance and confidence, and then success is sure.

Mark Twain

It's not enough to succeed. Others must fail.

Gore Vidal

See also *ACTION, CELEBRITY, CONFIDENCE,
FAILURE, FAME, RICHES, TALENT, WORK*

Suffering

By suffering comes wisdom.

Aeschylus

No pain—no gain.

Anonymous

Over the long run, he who suffers, conquers.

Anonymous

Man cannot remake himself without suffering.
For he is both the marble and the sculptor.

Alexis Carrel

Wounds heal and become scars, but scars grow
with us.

Stanislaw Lec

I do not believe that sheer suffering teaches. If
suffering alone taught, all the world would be

wise, since everyone suffers. To suffering must
be added mourning, understanding, patience,
love, openness and the willingness to remain
vulnerable.

Anne Morrow Lindbergh

Know how sublime a thing it is
To suffer and be strong.

Henry Wadsworth Longfellow

It is not true that suffering ennobles the character;
happiness does that sometimes, but suffering, for
the most part, makes men petty and vindictive.

W. Somerset Maugham

Man, the bravest of the animals and the one most
inured to suffering.

Friedrich Wilhelm Nietzsche

No pain, no palm; no thorns, no throne; no gall,
no glory; no cross, no crown.

William Penn

To suffer and to endure is the lot of humanity.

Pope Leo XIII

To live is also to suffer.

Mary Roberts Rinehart

He's truly valiant who can suffer wisely.

William Shakespeare: Timon of Athens

Misfortunes one can endure—they come from outside, they are accidents. But to suffer for one's own faults—ah—there is the sting of life.

Oscar Wilde

Misfortune and suffering is the only true international currency the world has ever had.

Max Wylie

See also GRIEF, SORROW, TROUBLES

Talent

In this world people have to pay an extortionate price for any exceptional gift whatever.

Willa Cather

Genius must have talent as its complement and implement.

Samuel Taylor Coleridge

Talent

Every natural power exhilarates; a true talent
delights the possessor first.

Ralph Waldo Emerson

There is no substitute for talent. Industry and all
virtues are of no avail.

Aldous Huxley

Everyone has talent. What is rare is the courage to
follow the talent to the dark place where it leads.

Erica Jong

I think this is the most extraordinary collection of
talent, of human knowledge, that has ever been
gathered together at the White House, with the
possible exception of when Thomas Jefferson
dined alone.

John F. Kennedy

It's a great talent to be able to conceal one's
talents.

François de La Rochefoucauld

*See also ACTING, FILM, GENIUS, HOLLYWOOD,
SUCCESS, TELEVISION*

Talk

So much they talked, so very little said.

Charles Churchill

Though I'm anything but clever,
I could talk like that for ever

Sir William S. Gilbert

We talk little, if we do not talk about ourselves.

William Hazlitt

Talking is a disease of age.

Ben Jonson

A gossip is one who talks to you about others: a
bore is one who talks to you about himself: a
brilliant conversationalist is one who talks to you
about yourself.

Lisa Kirk

If Thomas Jefferson had heard us, he probably
would have said, "We shouldn't have free speech."

Robin Quivers

Talk

Few men make themselves masters of the things they write or speak.

John Selden

All natural talk is a festival of ostentation . . . each accepts and fans the vanity of the other.

Robert Louis Stevenson

See also CONVERSATION, LANGUAGE, SILENCE, WORDS

Taste

Vulgarity is the garlic in the salad of taste.

James Brendan Connelly

You can't get high aesthetic tastes, like trousers, ready made.

Sir William S. Gilbert

Taste is the literary conscience of the soul.

Joseph Joubert

Every one as they like, as the woman said when she kissed her cow.

François Rabelais

Taste is the *only* morality . . . Tell me what you like, and I'll tell you what you are.

John Ruskin

A man of great common sense and good taste, meaning thereby a man without originality or moral courage.

George Bernard Shaw

You had no taste when you married me.

Richard Brinsley Sheridan

Taxes

To tax and to please, no more than to love and be wise, is not given to man.

Edmund Burke

There is one difference between a tax collector and a taxidermist—the taxidermist leaves the hide.

Mortimer Caplan

The art of taxation consists in so plucking the goose as to obtain the largest amount of feathers with the least possible amount of hissing.

J. B. Colbert

Taxes

. . . In this world nothing is certain but death and taxes.

Benjamin Franklin

Taxes are what we pay for civilized society.

Oliver Wendell Holmes, Jr.

Taxation without representation is tyranny.

James Otis

See also BUSINESS, DEBT, MONEY

Television

Television is called a medium because nothing is well done.

Goodman Ace

Television is a kind of radio which lets people at home see what the studio audience is not laughing at.

Fred Allen

Chewing gum for the eyes.

John Mason Brown

Moral passion without entertainment is propaganda, and entertainment without moral passion is television.

Rita Mae Brown

Television is an amusement park . . . we're in the boredom-killing business.

Paddy Chayefsky

You have debased [my] child. You have made him a laughingstock of intelligence . . . a stench in the nostrils of the ionosphere.

Lee DeForest

My idea of a good television mystery is one where it's hard to detect the sponsor.

Irv Lieberman

Television: Summer stock in an iron lung.

Beatrice Lillie

Television in its present form . . . [is] the opiate of the people of the United States.

Richard Nixon

Television

The doors to public proceedings should be
opened to television whenever they are open to
other elements of the press.

Robert W. Sarnoff

I hate television. I hate it as much as peanuts. But
I can't stop eating peanuts.

Orson Welles

Television is the source of our most powerful col-
lective memories.

Michael Winshop

Television is the world's most global language.

Michael Winshop

See also ACTING, DRAMA, HOLLYWOOD, TALENT

Temptation

The last temptation is the greatest treason:
To do the right deed for the wrong reason.

T. S. Eliot

Watch ye and pray, lest ye enter into temptation.
The spirit truly is ready, but the flesh is weak.

Mark 14:38

... Lead us not into temptation ...

Matthew 6:13

I am that way going to temptation,
Where prayers cross.

William Shakespeare: Measure for Measure

Never resist temptation: prove all things: hold fast
that which is good.

George Bernard Shaw

There are several good protections against temptations, but the surest is cowardice.

Mark Twain

Do you really think that it is weakness that yields
to temptations? I tell you that there are terrible
temptations which it requires strength, strength
and courage, to yield to.

Oscar Wilde

I can resist everything except temptation.

Oscar Wilde

The only way to get rid of a temptation is to
yield to it.

Oscar Wilde

Thought

Perish the thought!

Colley Cibber

To think is to live.

Cicero

Cogito, ergo sum. [I think, therefore I am.]

René Descartes

In fact, it is as difficult to appropriate the thoughts of others as it is to invent.

Ralph Waldo Emerson

Among mortals second thoughts are the wisest.

Euripides

First thoughts are best, being those of generous impulse; whereas Second Thoughts are those of Selfish Prudence.

Edward Fitzgerald

The thoughts that come often unsought, and, as it were, drop into the mind, are commonly the most valuable of any we have.

John Locke

My thought is me: that's why I can't stop. I exist
by what I think . . . and I can't prevent myself
from thinking.

Jean-Paul Sartre

Yon Cassius has a lean and hungry look;
He thinks too much: such men are dangerous.

William Shakespeare: Julius Caesar

I think, but I dare not speak.

William Shakespeare: Macbeth

Strange thoughts beget strange deeds.

Percy Bysshe Shelley

A penny for your thoughts.

Jonathan Swift

Great thoughts come from the heart.

Marquis de Vauvenargues

When a thought is too weak to be expressed simply, it is a proof that it should be rejected.

Marquis de Vauvenargues

See also *IDEAS, INTELLIGENCE, MIND, REASON*

Time

For thogh we slepe or wake, or rome, or ryde,
Ay fleeth the thyme, it nyl no man abyde.

Geoffrey Chaucer

My days are swifter than a weaver's shuttle . . .

Job 7:6

Consider, sir, how insignificant this will appear a
twelve-month hence.

Samuel Johnson

Tempus fugit. [Time flies.]

Ovid

Time rolls his ceaseless course.

Sir Walter Scott

Time: that which man is always trying to kill, but
which ends in killing him.

Herbert Spencer

I hate all times, because all times do fly
So fast away, and may not stayed be.

Edmund Spenser

See also AGE

Travel

I am astonished by people who want to "know" the universe when it's hard enough to find your way around Chinatown.

Woody Allen

The scull is no traveler; the wise man stays at home.
Traveling is a fool's paradise.

Ralph Waldo Emerson

If you reject the food, ignore the customs, fear the religion and avoid the people, you might better stay home.

James Michener

Everywhere is nowhere. When a person spends all his time in foreign travel, he ends by having many acquaintances, but no friends.

Seneca

I travel not to go anywhere, but to go.

Robert Louis Stevenson

To travel hopefully is a better thing than to arrive.

Robert Louis Stevenson

Travel

Always roaming with a hungry heart.

Alfred Lord Tennyson

I have traveled a good deal in Concord.

Henry David Thoreau

It is not worth while to go round the world to count the cats in Zanzibar.

Henry David Thoreau

See also JOURNEYS

Troubles

It is pleasant to recall past troubles.

Cicero

Chaos is a friend of mine.

Bob Dylan

This I know—if all men should take their trouble to market to barter with their neighbors, not one when he had seen the troubles of other men but would be glad to carry his own home again.

Herodotus

Man is born unto trouble, as the sparks fly upward.

Job 5:7

Man that is born of a woman is of few days, and full of trouble.

Job 14:1

The only incurable troubles of the rich are the troubles that money can't cure, which is a kind of trouble that is even more troublesome if you are poor.

Ogden Nash

Double, double, toil and trouble;
Fire burn and cauldron bubble.

William Shakespeare: Macbeth

If you're in trouble, you're alone.

Ross Thomas

See also HARDSHIP, SUFFERING

Trust

You may be deceived if you trust too much, but you will live in torment if you do not trust enough.

Frank Crane

Trust everybody, but cut the cards.

Finley Peter Dunne

Never trust the man who hath reason to suspect that you know he hath injured you.

Henry Fielding

Trust him no further than you can throw him.

Thomas Fuller

There is a Russian saying: *doveryai no proveryai*, trust but verify.

Mikhail Gorbachev

It is better never to trust anybody.

Henrik Ibsen

It is better to suffer wrong than to do it, and happier to be sometimes cheated than not to trust.

Samuel Johnson

Trust, like the soul, never returns, once it is gone.

Publilius Syrus

See also BELIEFS

Truth

Truth is such a rare thing, it is delightful to tell it.

Emily Dickinson

God offers to every mind its choice between
truth and repose.

Ralph Waldo Emerson

A writer is congenitally unable to tell the truth,
and that is why we call what he writes fiction.

William Faulkner

You have to remember: the truth is funny.

Timothy Leary

All truths that are kept silent become poison.

Friedrich Wilhelm Nietzsche

Sometimes we have to change the truth in order
to remember it.

George Santayana

Truth

Uninterpreted truth is as useless as buried gold.

Lytton Strachey

When in doubt, tell the truth.

Mark Twain

See also ADVICE, CRITICISM

Understanding

If one does not understand a person, one tends to regard him as a fool.

Carl Jung

. . . Get wisdom; and with all thy getting get understanding.

Proverbs 4:7

To understand everything makes one very indulgent.

Madame de Stäel

Universe

For the first time, the first, I laid my heart open to the benign indifference of the universe. To feel it

so like myself, indeed, so brotherly, made me realize that I'd been happy, and that I was happy still.

Albert Camus

. . . Listen; there's a hell
of a good universe next door; let's go.

e. e. cummings

Know that you are a part of the whole scheme of
things—a part of the universe.

Buckminster Fuller

The universe begins to look more like a great
thought than like a great machine.

Sir James Jeans

Taken as a whole, the universe is absurd.

Walter Savage Landor

The universe is one of God's thoughts.

Friedrich von Schiller

See also WORLD

Vanity

Vanity, like murder, will out.

Hannah Cowley

I have seen all the works that are done under the sun; and behold, all is vanity and vexation of spirit.

Ecclesiastes 1:14

A vain man can never be utterly ruthless; he wants to win applause and therefore he accommodates himself to others.

Johann Wolfgang von Goethe

What makes the vanity of other people insupportable is that it wounds our own.

François de La Rochefoucauld

Cruelty was the vice of the ancient, vanity is that of the modern world. Vanity is the last disease.

George Moore

Vanity, vanity, all is vanity
That's any fun at all for humanity.

Ogden Nash

One will rarely err if extreme actions be ascribed to vanity, ordinary actions to habit, and mean actions to fear.

Friedrich Wilhelm Nietzsche

Life without vanity is almost impossible.

Leo Tolstoy

See also CONCEIT, EGO, FASHION

Vice

Vice may be had at all prices.

Sir Thomas Browne

The greatest part of human gratifications approach nearly to vice.

Samuel Johnson

We are often saved from exclusive addiction to a single vice by the possession of others.

François de La Rochefoucauld

When the vices give us up, we flatter ourselves that we are giving them up.

François de La Rochefoucauld

Vice

I prefer an accommodating vice to an obstinate virtue.

Molière

The road to vice is not only downhill, but steep.

Seneca

What were once vices are now the manners of the day.

Seneca

Vice is a waste of life. Poverty, obedience, and celibacy are the canonical vices.

George Bernard Shaw

See also CRIME, EVIL, VIRTUE

Virtue

Virtue is like a rich stone—best plain set.

Francis Bacon

Virtue, enlightened, can be as calculating as vice.

Honoré de Balzac

A virtue to be serviceable must, like gold, be alloyed with some commoner but more durable metal.

Samuel Butler

Virtue has always been conceived of as victorious resistance to one's vital desire.

James Branch Cabell

Virtue is its own reward.

John Dryden

(Cicero, Seneca, Ovid, Philo, Claudian, Carlyle, and Emerson also expressed this aphorism.)

If he does really think there is no distinction between virtue and vice, why, sir, when he leave our houses let us count our spoons.

Samuel Johnson

In social life, we please more often by our vices than our virtues.

François de La Rochefoucauld

Virtue is a kind of health, beauty, and good habit of the soul.

Plato

Virtue

Assume a virtue, if you have it not.

William Shakespeare: Hamlet

Virtue itself of vice must pardon beg.

William Shakespeare: Hamlet

Some rise by sin, and some by virtue fall.

William Shakespeare: Measure for Measure

Be good, and you will be lonesome.

Mark Twain

Virtue is the compensation to the poor for the want of riches.

Horace Walpole

See also EVIL, RIGHT, VICE

War

An infallible method of conciliating a tiger is to allow oneself to be devoured.

Konrad Adenauer

War must be for the sake of peace.

Aristotle

War would end if the dead could return.

Stanley Baldwin

There are no warlike peoples, just warlike leaders.

Ralph Bunche

War is too important to be left to the generals.

Georges Clemenceau

Peace itself is war in masquerade.

John Dryden

War is sweet to those who have not experienced it.

Erasmus

There never was a good war or a bad peace.

Benjamin Franklin

You should never wear your best trousers when
you go out to fight for liberty and truth.

Herbert Gibson

War is only a cowardly escape from the problems
of peace.

Thomas Mann

War

The same reasons that make us quarrel with a neighbor cause war between two princes.

Michel de Montaigne

There is no squabbling so violent as that between people who accepted an idea yesterday and those who will accept it tomorrow.

Christopher Morley

Whoever battled with monsters had better see that it does not turn him into a monster. And if you gaze long in an abyss, the abyss will gaze back into you.

Friedrich Wilhelm Nietzsche

War can only be abolished through war.

Mao Tse-tung

To be prepared for war is one of the most effectual means of preserving peace.

George Washington

One of our American wits said that it took only half as long to train an American army as any other because you only had to train them to go one way.

Woodrow Wilson

See also ANGER, ENEMIES, HEROISM, PEACE

Wisdom

We thought, because we had power, we had wisdom.

Stephen Vincent Benét

All human wisdom is summed up in two words— wait and hope.

Alexandre Dumas, père

Wisdom never lies.

Homer

Wisdom is early to repair.

Gerard Manley Hopkins

The only medicine for suffering, crime, and all the other woes of mankind, is wisdom.

Thomas Henry Huxley

Wisdom

The price of wisdom is above rubies.

Job 28:18

The fear of the Lord is the beginning of wisdom.

Psalms 111:10

One may almost doubt if the wisest man has learned anything of absolute value by living.

Henry David Thoreau

See also KNOWLEDGE

Wives

He that hath wife and children hath given hostages to fortune; for they are impediments to great enterprises, either of virtue, or mischief.

Francis Bacon

Wives are young men's mistresses, companions for middle age, and old men's nurses.

Francis Bacon

Man's best possession is a loving wife.

Robert Burton

To take a wife merely as an agreeable and rational companion will commonly be found to be a grand mistake.

Lord Chesterfield

What a pity it is that nobody knows how to manage a wife but a bachelor.

George Colman the Elder

I want a girl just like the girl that married dear old dad.

William Dillon

The comfortable estate of widowhood, is the only hope that keeps up a wife's spirits.

John Gay

The only comfort of my life
Is that I never yet had wife

Robert Herrick

Whoso findeth a wife findeth a good thing.

Proverbs 18:22

It is a good horse than never stumbles,
And a good wife that never grumbles.

John Ray

Wives

My dear, my better half.

Sir Philip Sidney

The real business of a fall is to look out for a wife, to look after a wife, or to look after somebody else's wife.

Robert Smith Surtees

See also HUSBANDS, MARRIAGE, WOMAN

Woman

Pregnancy is an occupational hazard of being a wife. It is a very boring time. I'm not particuarly maternal.

Anne, Princess Royal

. . . can't live with them, or without them.

Aristophanes

One is not born a woman; one becomes one.

Simone de Beauvoir

Woman would be more charming if one could fall into her arms without falling into her hands.

Ambrose Bierce

The trouble with some women is they get all excited about nothing—and then they marry him.

Cher

Woman: one of nature's agreeable blunders.

Hannah Cowley

Let us look for the woman.

Alexandre Dumas, père

In your amours you should prefer old women to young ones. They are so grateful!

Benjamin Franklin

Women like to sit down with trouble as if it were knitting.

Ellen Glasgow

I didn't know until recently that women were supposed to be inferior.

Katharine Hepburn

There are two ways to handle a woman, and nobody knows either of them.

Kin (Frank McKinney) Hubbard

Woman

The two divinest things this world has got,
A lovely woman in a rural spot.

Leigh Hunt

For the Colonel's Lady an' Judy O'Grady
Are sisters under their skins!

Rudyard Kipling

One can find women who have never had one
love affair, but it is rare indeed to find any who
have had only one.

François de La Rochefoucauld

Being a woman is of special interest only to aspir-
ing male transexuals. To actual women, it is merely
an excuse not to play football.

Fran Lebowitz

I'm furious about the Women's Liberationists.
They keep getting up on soapboxes and proclaim-
ing that women are brighter than men. That's
true, but it should be kept quiet or it ruins the
whole racket.

Anita Loos

The highest prize in the world of men is to have the most beautiful woman available on your arm, and living there, in her heart always loyal to you.

Norman Mailer

Woman is unrestrainable, unguidable, intractable, undrawable, unleadable, harsh, bitter, austere, and implacable.

Menander

The natural superiority of woman is a biological fact, and a socially acknowledged reality.

Ashley Montague

Woman was God's *second* mistake.

Friedrich Wilhelm Nietzsche

The vote means nothing to women. We should be armed.

Edna O'Brien

When the candles are out all women are fair.

Plutarch

But every woman is at heart a rake.

Alexander Pope

Woman

A woman is like a tea bag. You don't know her strength until she is in hot water.

Nancy Reagan

Women prefer us to say a little evil of them, rather than say nothing at all.

Louis Xavier de Ricard

Lady, you are the cruel'st she alive.

William Shakespeare: Twelfth Night

Like all young men, you greatly exaggerate the difference between one young woman and another.

George Bernard Shaw

A woman without a man is like a fish without a bicycle.

Gloria Steinem

Now, we are becoming the men we wanted to marry.

Gloria Steinem

Women deserve to have more than twelve years between the ages of twenty-eight and forty.

James Thurber

Once a woman has given you her heart, you can never get rid of the rest of her.

Sir John Vanbrugh

If it's a woman, it's caustic; if it's a man, it's authoritative.

Barbara Walters

People call me a feminist whenever I express sentiments that differentiate me from a doormat or a prostitute.

Rebecca West

Woman is like the reed, which bends in every breeze, but breaks not in the tempest.

Richard Whately

See also MAN, MARRIAGE, WIVES

Words

A blow with a word strikes deeper than a blow with a sword.

Robert Burton

You can get a lot more done with a kind word and a gun, than with a kind word alone.

Al Capone

"The question is," said Alice, "whether you can make words mean so many different things."
"The question is," said Humpty Dumpty, "which is to be master—that's all."

Lewis Carroll

Of all cold words of tongue or pen
The worst are these: "I knew him when"

Arthur Guiterman

How forcible are right words!

Job 6:25

Words are, of course, the most powerful drug used by mankind.

Rudyard Kipling

Every word is a preconceived judgment.

Friedrich Nietzche

Critics search for ages for the wrong word, which, to give them credit, they eventually find.

Peter Ustinov

What's another word for Thesaurus?

Steven Wright

See also AUTHORS, BOOKS, CREATIVITY, EDUCATION, LEARNING, LETTERS, LITERATURE, READING, TALK

Work

All work, even cotton spinning, is noble; work is alone noble.

Thomas Carlyle

Blessed is he who has found his work; let him ask no other blessedness.

Thomas Carlyle

Housework can't kill you, but why take a chance?

Phyllis Diller

Work

By working faithfully eight hours per day, you may eventually get to be a boss and work twelve hours a day.

Robert Frost

All work and no play makes Jack a dull boy.

James Howell

Better to work and fail than to sleep one's life away.

Jerome K. Jerome

There's no place where success comes before work, except in the dictionary.

Donald Kimball

For men must work, and women must weep,
And there's little to earn and many to keep . . .

Charles Kingsley

Work expands so as to fill the time available for its completion and the thing to be done swells in importance and complexity in a direct ratio with the time to be spent.

C. Northcote Parkinson

World

You may tempt the upper classes
With your villainous demitasses,
But Heaven will protect the working girl.

Edgar Smith

Work consists of whatever a body is obliged to do
. . . Play consists of whatever a body is not obliged
to do.

Mark Twain

Work keeps us from three great evils, boredom,
vice and need.

Voltaire

Work is the curse of the drinking class.

Oscar Wilde

See also *ABILITY, ACCOMPLISHMENT, ACHIEVE-
MENT, AMBITION, JOBS, LAZINESS, SUCCESS*

World

To see a world in a grain of sand . . .

William Blake

World

...The world, the flesh, and the devil.

The Book of Common Prayer

The world, which took but six days to make, is like to take six thousand to make out.

Sir Thomas Browne

This may not be the best of all possible worlds, but to say that it is the worst is mere petulant nonsense.

Thomas Henry Huxley

The world, where much is to be done and little to be known.

Samuel Johnson

O brave new world.

William Shakespeare: The Tempest

This world is a comedy to those that think, a tragedy to those that feel.

Horace Walpole

See also UNIVERSE

Youth

I'm not young enough to know everything.

Sir James M. Barrie

When the waitress puts the dinner on the table, the old men look at the dinner. The young men look at the waitress.

Gelett Burgess

Almost everything that is great has been done by youth.

Benjamin Disraeli

Youth is a blunder; manhood a struggle; old age a regret.

Benjamin Disraeli

Youth is the best time to be rich, and the best time to be poor.

Euripides

Youth's a stuff will not endure.

William Shakespeare: Twelfth Night

Youth

Youth is wasted on the young.

George Bernard Shaw

If every day is an awakening, you will never grow old. You will just keep growing.

Gail Sheehy

No wise man ever wished to be younger.

Jonathan Swift

See also ADOLESCENCE, AGE, CHILDREN, DEATH

Index of Topics

Index of Topics

Index of Topics

Index of Topics

Index of Topics

Index of Topics

Index of Topics

Index of Sources

Index of Sources

Index of Sources

Index of Sources

Index of Sources

Chesterton, G. K.—Death, Education, Evil, Failure, Faith, Fate, Intelligence, Language, Laughter, Literature

Chevalier, Maurice—Age

Child, Julia—Food

Chinese proverb—Riches, Sorrow

Chuang-Tzu—Knowledge

Churchill, Charles—Talk

Churchill, Winston—Alcohol, Convictions, Diplomats, Goodwill, Learning, Lying

Cibber, Colley—Thought

Cicero—Age, Books, Deprecation, Grief, Leisure, Manners, Pleasure, Self, Thought, Troubles

Cioran, E. M.—Ego, Fanaticism

Clarke, John—Love

Clarke, Tom—Children

Clay, Henry—Right

Clemenceau, Georges—War

Cleveland, Grover—Democracy

Cobbett, William—Poverty

Cocteau, Jean—Books, Films

Colbert, J. B.—Taxes

Coleridge, Samuel Taylor—Loneliness, Praise, Talent

Collie, G. Norman—Husbands

Collier, David—Books

Collins, John Churton—Friendship

Colman, George, the Elder—Wives

Colton, Charles Caleb—Imitation, Laws

Columbat—Knowledge

Confucius—Animals, Heart, Kindness, Life, Neighbor

Congreve, William—Music

Index of Sources

Index of Sources

Index of Sources

Goldwyn, Samuel—Films, Hollywood

Goodman, Benny—Prejudice

Goodman, Paul—Creativity

Gorbachev, Mikhail—Trust

Gould, Lawrence—Security

de Gourmont, Rémy—Beauty, Chastity

Gracián, Baltasar—Accomplishment, Bargains, Disease, Experience, Intelligence, Laughter

Graham, Martha—Body, Health

Grass, Günter—The Arts, Democracy

Gray, Thomas—Ignorance

Greeley, Horace—Bible

Green, Julian—Boredom

Greene, Robert—Contentment

Gregory, Dick—African-Americans, Liberal

Grentell, J.—Happiness

Greville, Richard Fulke—Intelligence

Grizzard, Lewis—Alimony

Grove, Andrew S.—Business

Guedalla, Phillip—History

Guinon, Albert—Solitude

Guisewite, Cathy—Food

Guiterman, Arthur—Words

Gypsy proverb—Riches

Hackett, Buddy—Diet

Haldane, J. B. S.—Future

Half, Robert—Ability

Lord Halifax—Accomplishment, Anger, Dreams, Fame, Hope, Learning, Opinions

Hall, James—Lying

Hall, Jerry—Love

Hammarskjöld, Dag—Beliefs

Index of Sources

Index of Sources

Index of Sources

Index of Sources

Index of Sources

Index of Sources

Index of Sources

Index of Sources

Index of Sources

Index of Sources

Index of Sources

Stevenson, Robert Louis—Bravery, Fear, Friendship, Life, Lying, Talk, Travel

Stimson, Henry L.— Hope

Stoppard, Tom—Age, Democracy

Strachey, Lytton—Truth

Stravinsky, Igor—The Arts, Future

Streisand, Barbra— Marriage

Sudermann, Hermann— Laughter, Listening

Sunday, Billy—Bible

Surtees, Robert Smith— Pleasure, Wives

Sutherland, George— Freedom

Sutton, David—Children, Life

Swetchine, Anne Sophie—Age

Swift, Jonathan—Advice, Afterlife, Age, Ambition,

Blindness, Celebrity, Disappointment, Evil, Genius, Happiness, History, Laws, Luck, Thought, Youth

Syrus, Publilius—Anger, Evil, Trust

Szasz, Thomas—Children, Definitions, Disease, Solitude

Tacitus—Blame, Power

de Talleyrand-Périgord, Charles Maurice— Friendship

The Talmud—Age, God

Tawney, Richard H.— History, Opportunity

Teasdale, Sara—Joy

Tennyson, Alfred Lord— Desperation, Friendship, Husbands, Ignorance, Kindness, Lying, Travel

Terence—Sex

Teshigahara, S.—Beauty

Thackeray, William Makepeace—Marriage, Pleasure

493

Index of Sources

Index of Sources

Index of Sources